Bradley's

How To Play Pop and Jazz Piano

Book One

by

Richard Bradley

© 1996 BRADLEY PUBLICATIONS
Exclusive Selling Agent Throughout the World: WARNER BROS. PUBLICATIONS U.S. INC., 15800 N.W. 48th Avenue, Miami, FL 33014
Any duplication, adaptation or arrangement of the compositions and/or text contained in this book requires the written consent of the Publisher. No part of this book may be photocopied or reproduced in any way without permission. Unauthorized uses are an infringement of the U.S. Copyright Act and are punishable by Law.

Song Listing

Preface

This text is for those who want to learn to play current pops as well as great standards, and develop skills in jazz improvisation, arranging and playing a variety of piano styles. All that is required to begin is a basic knowledge of music and early piano skills. *Bradley's How To Play Pop And Jazz Piano* can be used successfully in conjunction with the Bradley piano methods, or with any other standard or classical method of piano or keyboard study.

Some people think, you either have a talent for playing pop and jazz or you don't. The truth is, anyone can learn these styles. One classical piano teacher told me, "I don't play jazz because you must know so much about music." As with any type of music, the more musical knowledge we have, the more creative we can be.

In general, classical music is read and interpreted by the markings on the printed music. You are trying to recreate how the composer envisioned his or her work. In popular music and jazz, we become creators as well as players, either by improvising or arranging. This course was developed to give you all the theory, harmony and technical skills required to become a first rate popular or jazz musician, however, even if your interest is primarily in pop and jazz, I feel some study of classical piano is beneficial in developing sight-reading skills and playing technique.

It is important to cover each piece and exercise in this text. Do not skip from one piece to another, or just cherry-pick certain arrangements. The order is important because one style develops from another. For example, jazz and rock developed from blues.

You will notice there are many blues pieces in this volume. The idea is not just to play them, but to play enough to help your ear recognize chord changes. The same thing applies to chord progressions or Pat-Cors™ as we call them (a short term for "patterns of chords"). By naming the Pat-Cors™, and reinforcing them by playing them in many keys and different pieces, you will eventually be able to hear them before they occur.

The ear is an essential part of playing. **Listen** to as mush music as you can. Develop a library of recordings, tapes and CD's. If jazz is your thing, become familiar with several artists who are particularly strong in a certain style. Although these artists can play most styles, they have become known for a certain style or sound. George Shearing is known for his blocked style of chording doubling the melody in the left hand. McCoy Tyner has developed a unique sound with quartal harmony, chords built in fourths rather than thirds. Learn to **hear** the difference between Oscar Peterson, Dave Brubeck and Marion McPartland.

We have often heard jazz musicians singing along under their breath as they play. I'm not suggesting this, however singing an improvisation will often help us find the notes we want to play on the keyboard. Instead of singing "Happy birthday to you," sing: "Hap-idy birthday to you-be-do-be-do-be. Listening to the recording of Ella Fitzgerald will give you great insight into improvising as she "scat sings" the singing of nonsense syllables, "De-dab-ba-dee-do-ba."

Playing on electronic keyboards with accompanying rhythms or other tracks is an excellent way to develop your sense of rhythm. Always play at a tempo that allows you to keep a steady beat. If your tempo is so fast it makes you miss beats, or have uneven beats, stop and start again at a slower tempo you can keep even.

If you find you need more musical background or playing or reading skills, look at my adult piano course, *Bradley's How To Play Piano*, in book and/or video form.

Now it's time to get started and enjoy playing pop and jazz!

Richard Bradley

Intervals

An **interval**
is the distance between two notes.

Two notes sounded together form a **harmonic interval**.

Two notes played in succession form a **melodic interval**.

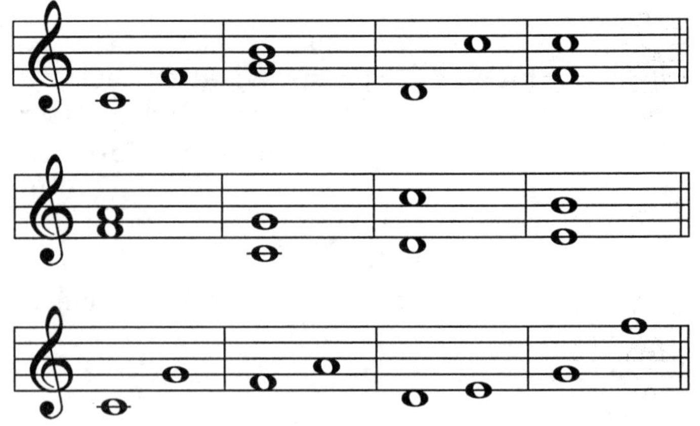

Intervals Formed on the Major Scale

Unison (Prime) | 2nd | 3rd | 4th | 5th | 6th | 7th | Octave

M2 | M3 | P4 | P5 | M6 | M7 | P8

2nds, 3rds, 6ths and 7ths are **major intervals**.
4ths, 5ths and octaves are **perfect intervals**.

Other Intervals

A major interval reduced by a half step is a **minor interval**.
A minor or perfect interval reduced by a half step is a **diminished interval**.
A major or perfect interval increased by a half step is an **augmented interval**.

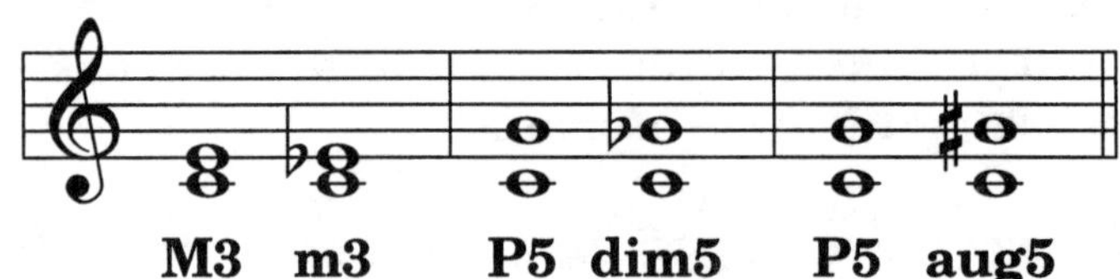

Complete each interval on the staff below:

Check the intervals you completed::

Draw the interval of a third above each note on the staff below, then play the example.

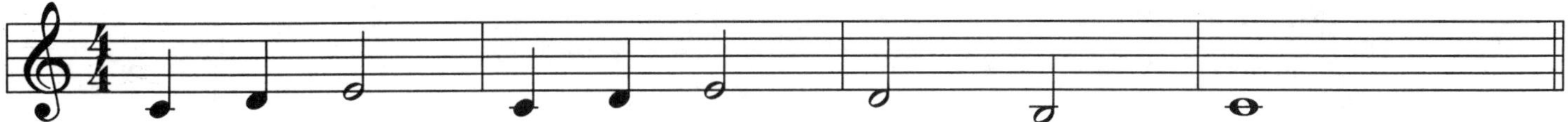

Draw the interval of a sixth above each note on the staff below, then play the example.

Name the left hand interval in the piece below. __________

Rock On The Dock

By RICHARD BRADLEY

© 1996 BRADLEY PUBLICATIONS
All Rights Reserved

In "Mariachi's Lullaby", the right hand plays intervals of a ______ except for the last two measures which is the interval of a ______.

Find and play the left hand bass pattern starting on C, next find and play it starting on F, then on G. Write the bass patterns starting on F and G on the staff below.

6th 2nd 5th

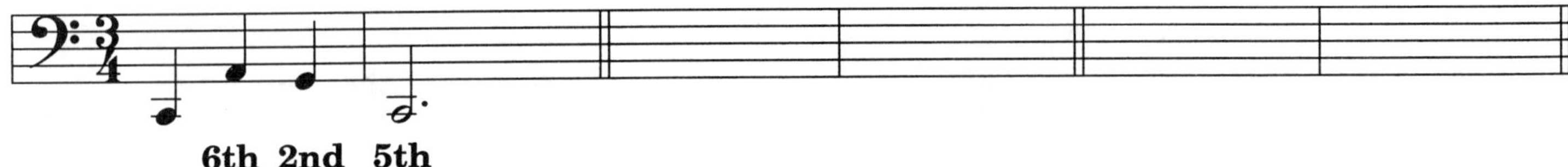

Mariachi's Lullaby

By RICHARD BRADLEY

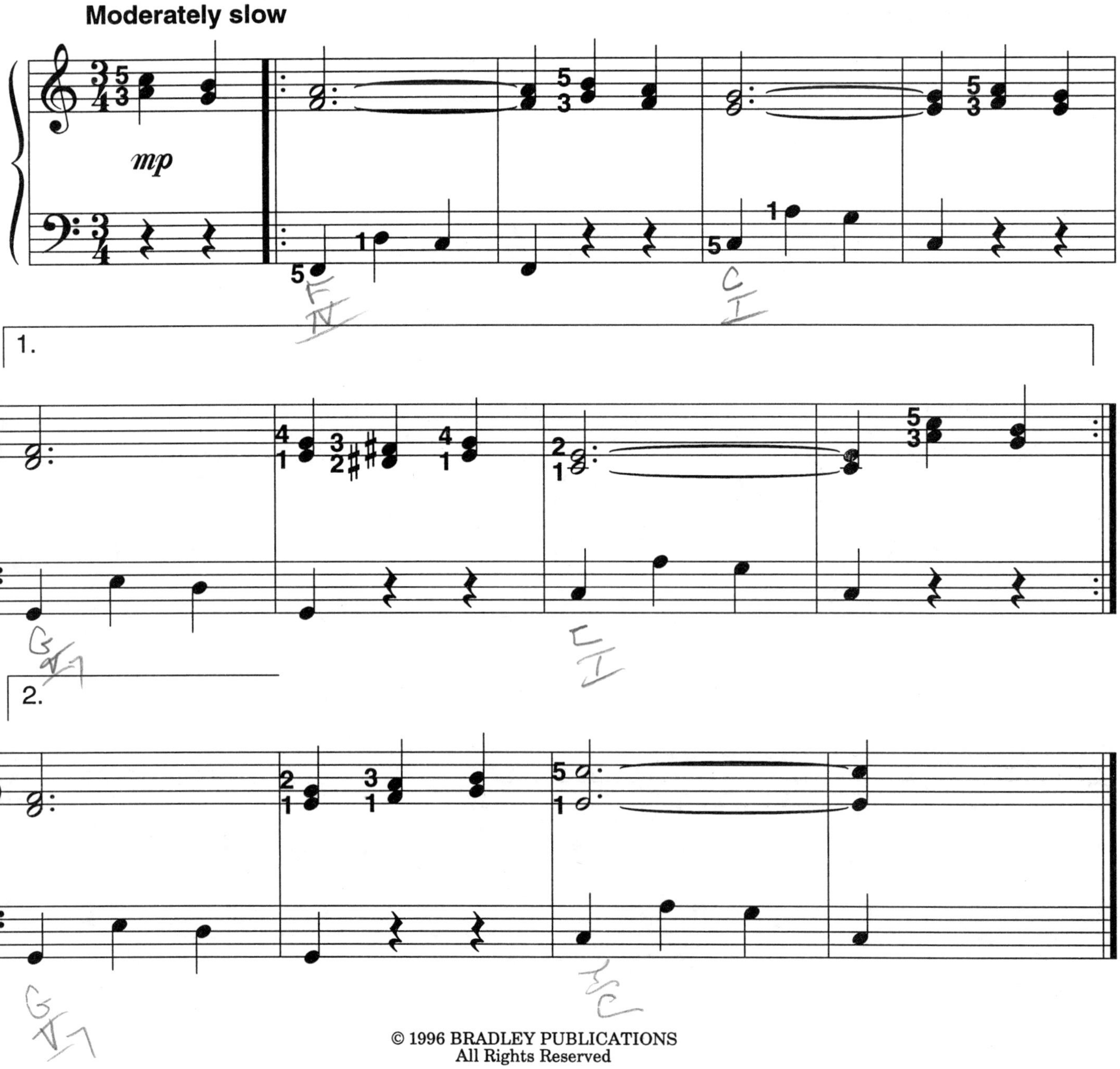

Moderately slow
mp
1.
2.

© 1996 BRADLEY PUBLICATIONS
All Rights Reserved

Eighth Notes

In rock and some popular music, eighth notes are played even and steady, the same as in classical music. We will learn jazz and swing rhythms later.

When you see the notes to the right indicating that two eighth notes equal two eighth notes, it means play them evenly.

Rock Steady

By RICHARD BRADLEY

© 1996 BRADLEY PUBLICATIONS
All Rights Reserved

The Beat Goes On

Words and Music by
SONNY BONO
Arranged by Richard Bradley

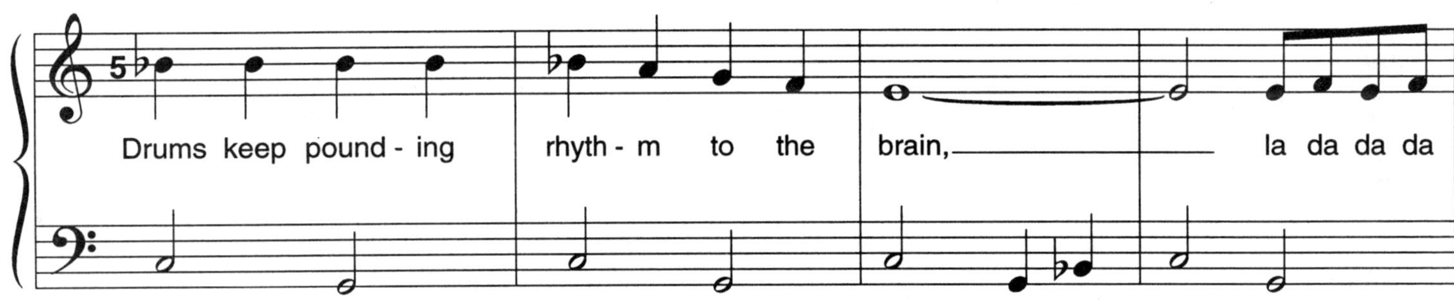

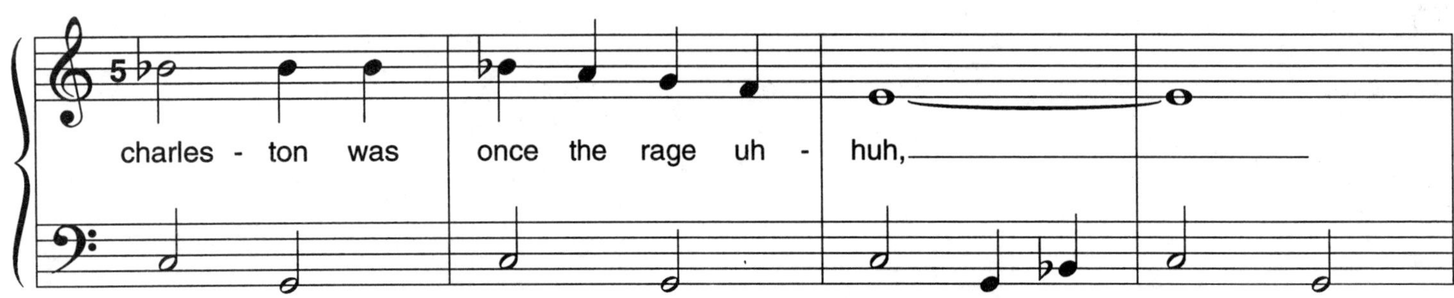

© 1967 (Renewed 1995) COTILLION MUSIC, INC. & CHRIS-MARC MUSIC
This arrangement © 1996 COTILLION MUSIC, INC. & CHRIS-MARC MUSIC
All rights administered by WARNER-TAMERLANE PUBLISHING CORP.
All Rights Reserved

4
his - to - ry has turned a page, uh - huh. The
3

min - i - skirt's the cur - rent thing, uh - huh,

4
teen - y bop-per is our new born king, uh - huh. And the beat goes
3

on, the beat goes on.

Chromatic Scale

The **chromatic scale** is made up of all half steps.
A half step goes from one key to the very next on the keyboard.

Left Hand Fingering

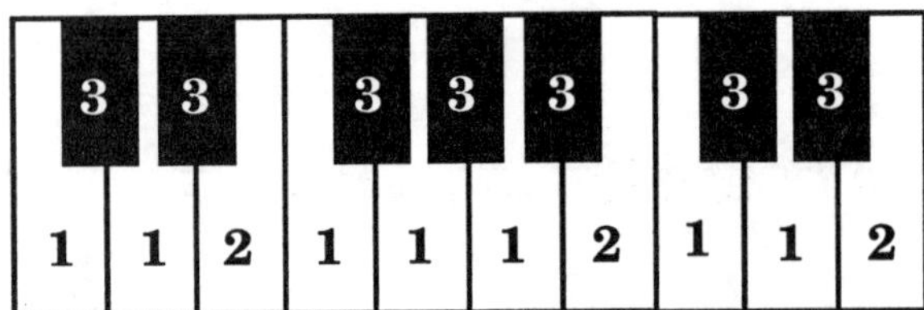

3rd finger plays all black keys.
2nd finger plays all E's and B's.
Thumb plays the remaining white keys.

Right Hand Fingering

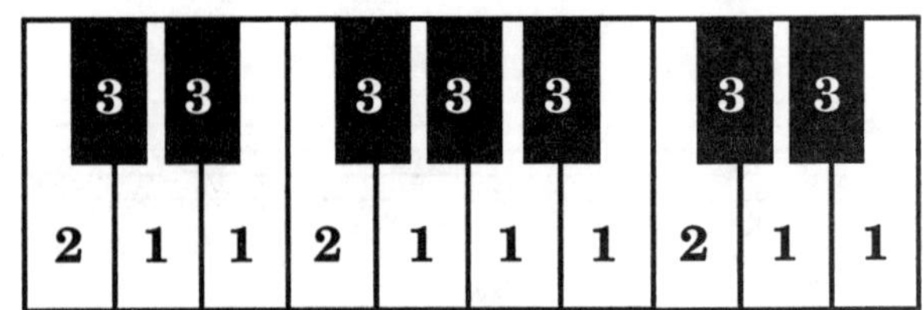

3rd finger plays all black keys.
2nd finger plays all C's and F's.
Thumb plays the remaining white keys.

Chromatic Blue

By RICHARD BRADLEY

© 1996 BRADLEY PUBLICATIONS
All Rights Reserved

The chromatic scale uses sharps ascending

and flats descending.

Chromatic Boogie

By RICHARD BRADLEY

Steady beat

© 1996 BRADLEY PUBLICATIONS
All Rights Reserved

Ragtime Rhythms

Ragtime is a style of American jazz that is characterized by a syncopated rhythm usually played slow with even eighth notes. Artists such as Scott Joplin made it extremely popular, bringing it to its peak of popularity between 1910 and 1915.

Syncopation occurs when a note is played before and after a beat, but not on the beat. In the example below, the syncopation occurs before and after the second beat.

Even Eighth Notes | **Syncopated Second Beat** | **Often Written This Way**

1 & 2 & 3 & 4 & | 1 & 2 & 3 & 4 & | 1 & 2 & 3 & 4 &

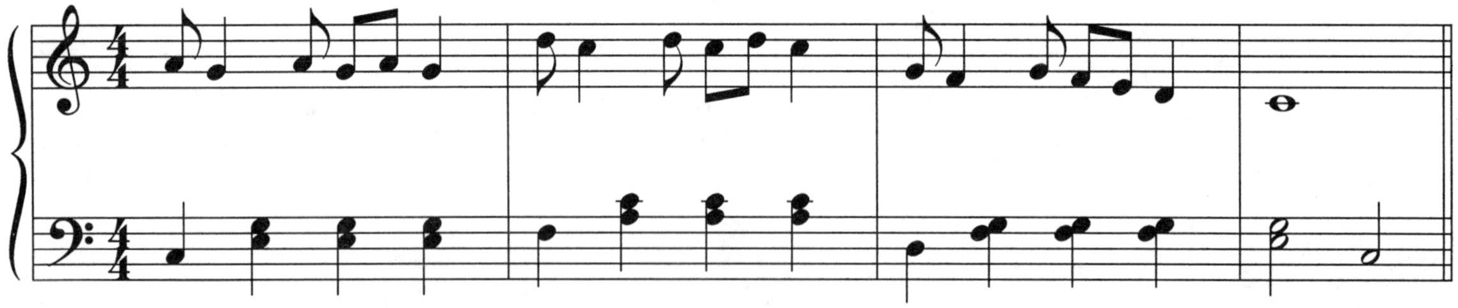

Even Eighth Notes | **Syncopated Third Beat**

1 & 2 & 3 & 4 & | 1 & 2 & 3 & 4 &

The Easy Winners

SCOTT JOPLIN
(1868 - 1917)
Arranged by Richard Bradley

11/16

Moderately slow

© 1996 BRADLEY PUBLICATIONS
All Rights Reserved

The Entertainer

SCOTT JOPLIN
(1868 - 1917)
Arranged by Richard Bradley

© 1996 BRADLEY PUBLICATIONS
All Rights Reserved

Chords

A **chord** is three or more notes sounded together.
A **triad** is a three note chord.
A **chord symbol**, which is usually found above the melody, is the name of the chord to be played.
The **root** is the note the chord is built on and its name.
Chords starting on their root are always written either all on lines or all on spaces on the staff.

Play the chords (triads) built on the C major scale.

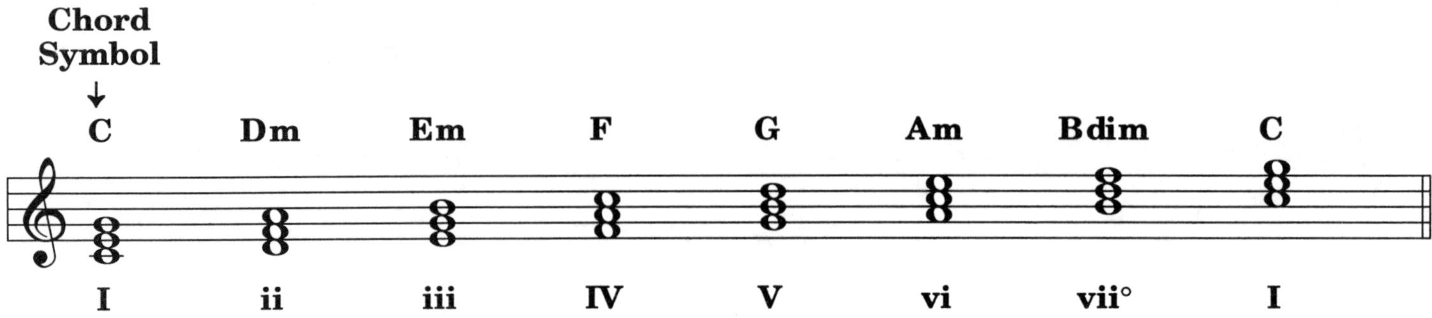

Major chords are formed by playing:
Root + 4 half steps above + 3 half steps above.

Major chords are found on the I, IV and V degrees of the major scale indicated with upper case Roman numerals.

Major chord symbols are just the letter name of the chord: C, F, B♭, etc.

Minor chords are formed by playing:
Root + 3 half steps above + 4 half steps above.
A minor chord can also be seen as a major chord with a lowered 3rd.

Minor chords are found on the ii, iii and vi degrees of the major scale indicated with lower case Roman numerals.

Minor chord symbols have the letter name with a lower case "m" for minor: Cm, Fm, E♭m, etc.

Diminished chords are formed by playing:
Root + 3 half steps above + 3 half steps above.
A diminished chord can also be seen as a major chord with a lowered 3rd and lowered 5th.

The diminished chord is found on the vii degree of the major scale indicated with a lower case Roman numeral followed by a degree sign "vii°".

Diminished chord symbols have the letter name followed by "dim" for diminished: Cdim, Fdim, A A♭dim, etc.

Play the chords of the major scale as broken chords.

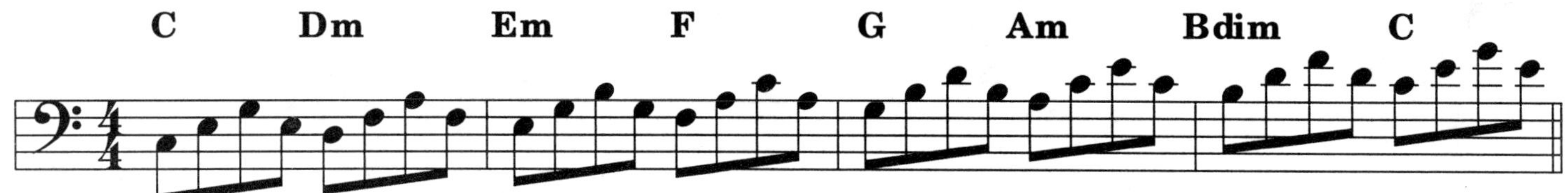

Play broken chords with your right hand and solid chords with your left hand.

Play solid chords with your left hand and scale tones starting on the root of each chord with your right hand.

The following examples use a pattern of alternating broken chords and scale tones.

Chord Progressions

A **chord progression** is a series of chords that follow one another. I will refer to these by the term Pat-Cor™ (pattern of chords). This will help you recognize each pattern.

Pat-Cor™ No. 1

This chord progression uses the first three chords of the major scale.

C – Dm – Em – Dm
(Key of C Major)

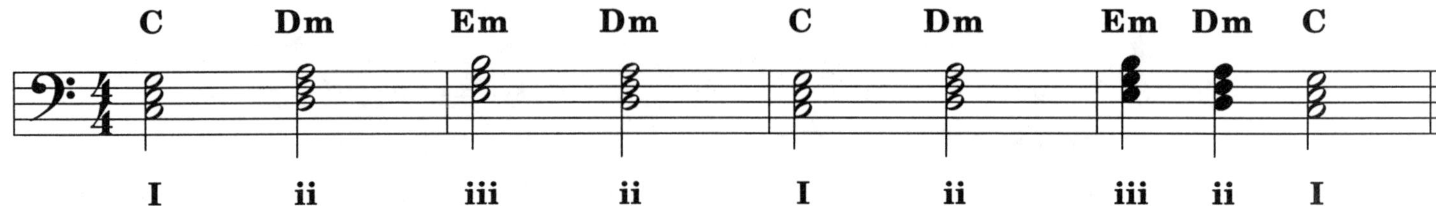

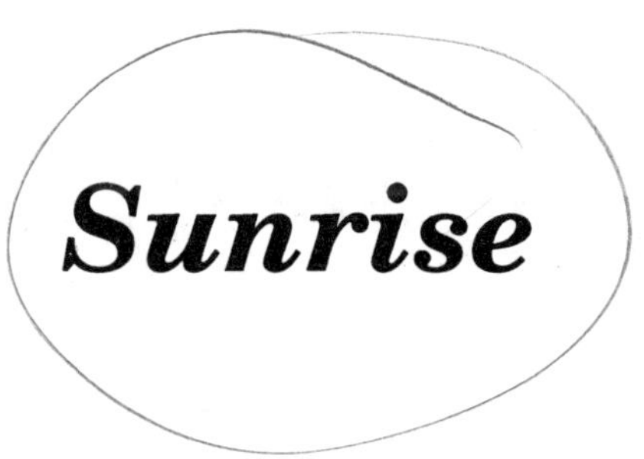

By RICHARD BRADLEY

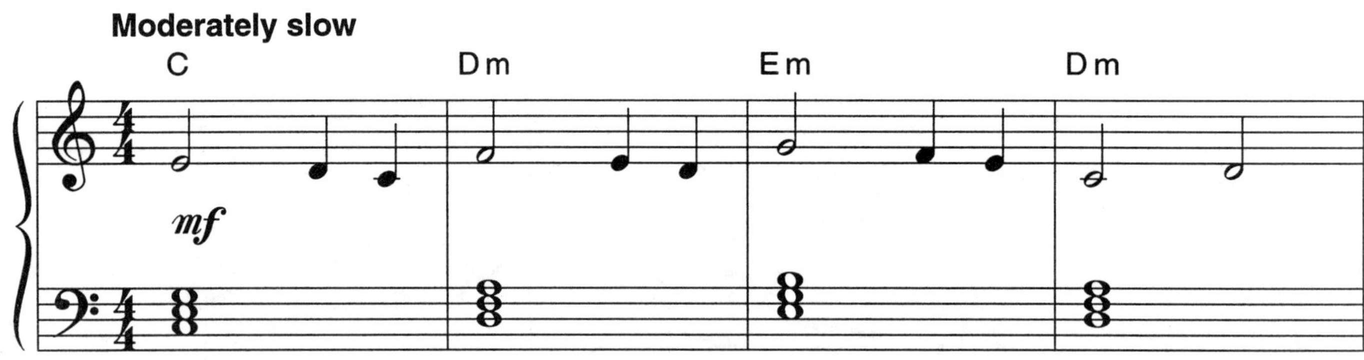

© 1996 BRADLEY PUBLICATIONS
All Rights Reserved

Write in the chords for Pat-Cor™ No. 1, then play the piece.

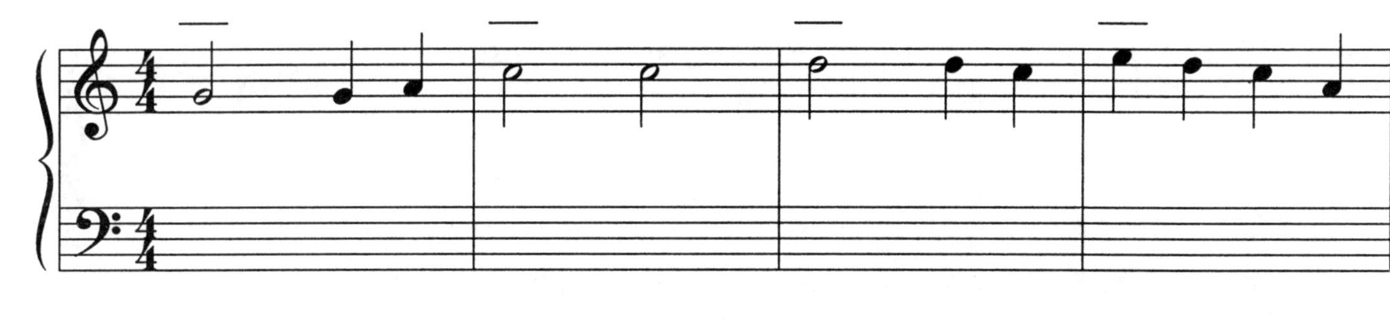

Are You Sleeping?

TRADITIONAL
Arranged by Richard Bradley

© 1996 BRADLEY PUBLICATIONS
All Rights Reserved

Rhythm Of The Rain

By
JOHN GUMMOE
Arranged by Richard Bradley

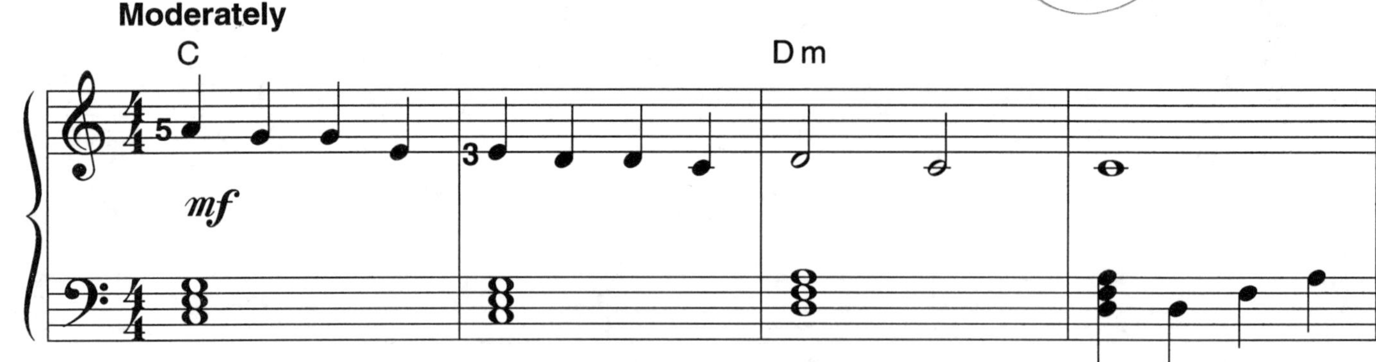

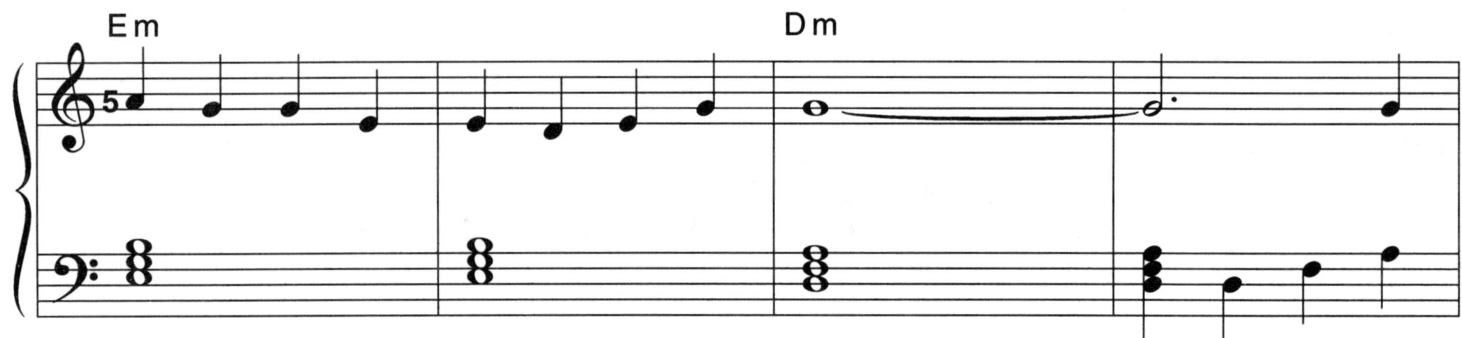

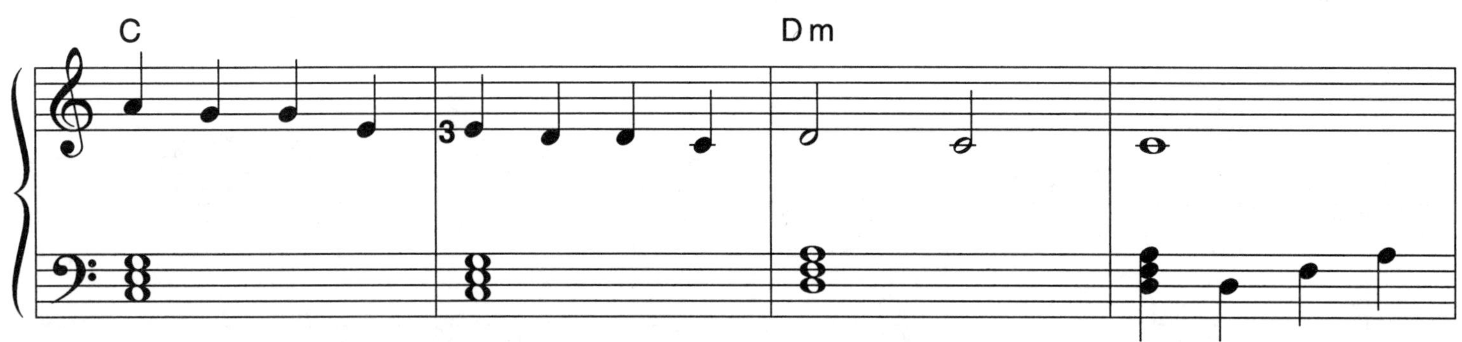

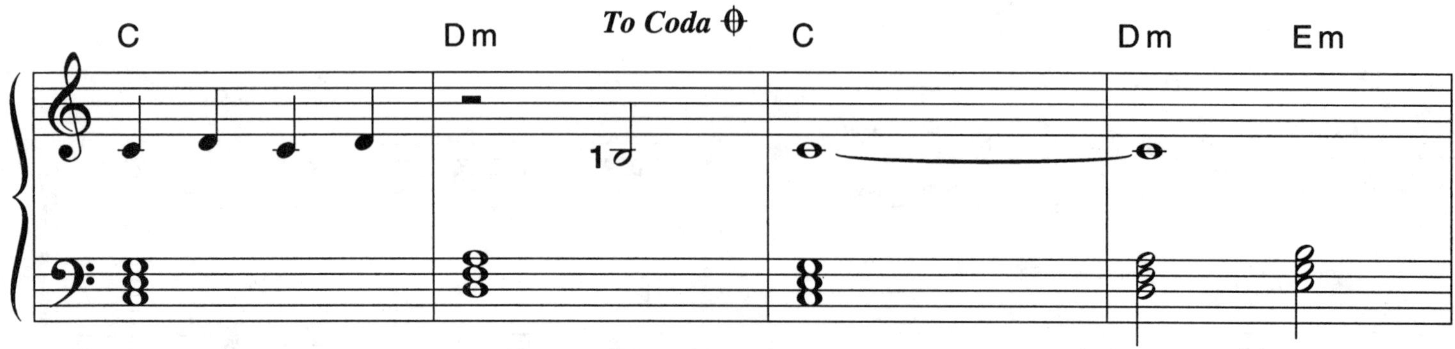

© 1962 (Renewed 1990) WARNER-TAMERLANE PUBLISHING CORP.
This arrangement © 1996 WARNER-TAMERLANE PUBLISHING CORP.
All Rights Reserved

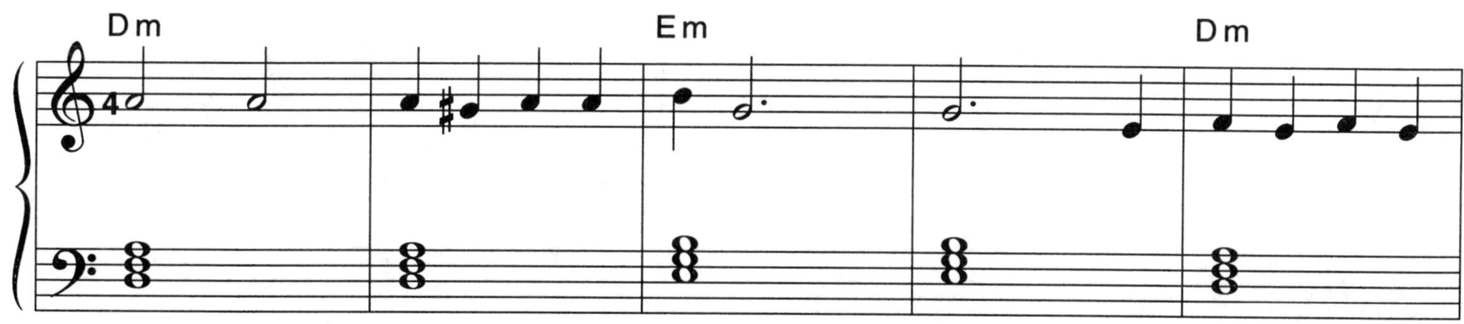
Dm
Em
Dm
4

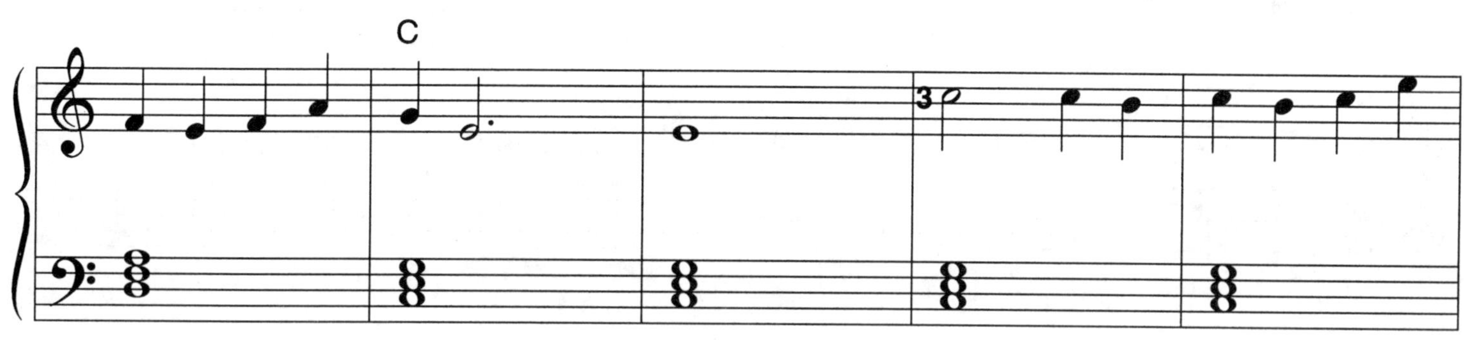
C
3

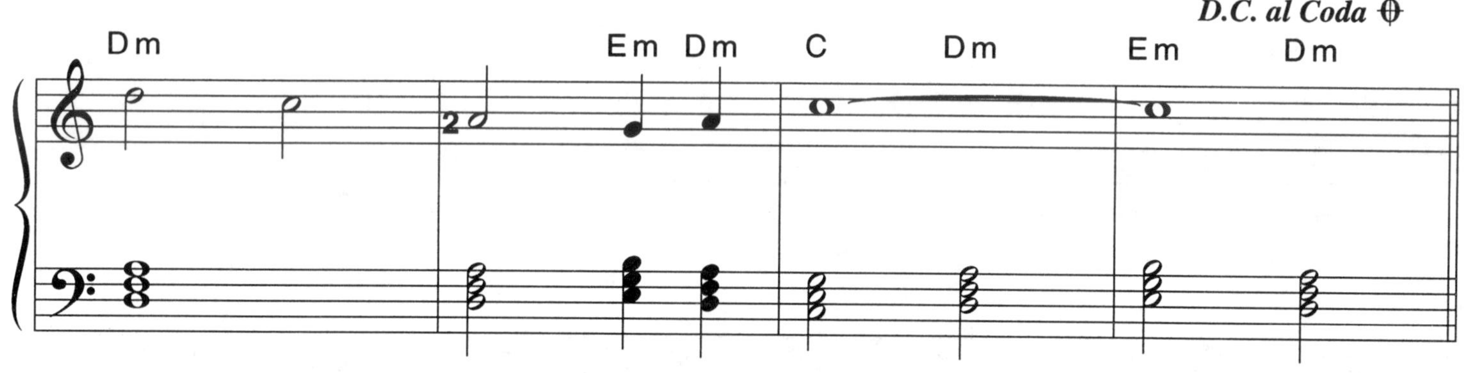
D.C. al Coda
Dm
Em Dm
C
Dm
Em
Dm
2

Coda
C
Dm
C
Dm
C
4

The Grandfather Clock

TRADITIONAL
Arranged by Richard Bradley

© 1996 BRADLEY PUBLICATIONS
All Rights Reserved

Remember, Pat-Cor™ No. 1 comes from the first three chords of a major scale.

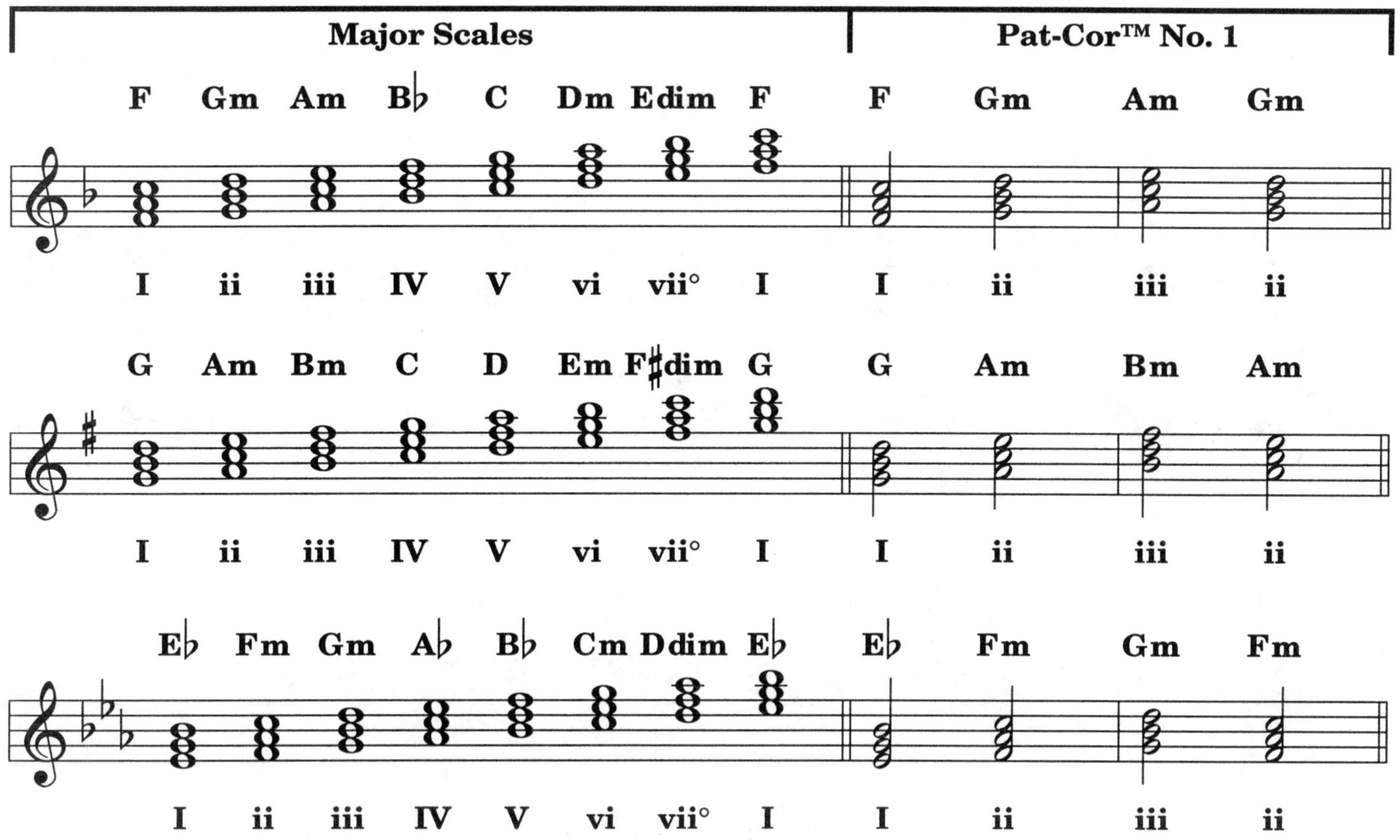

On the staffs below, write in the chords for the major scales of B♭, D, A and A♭, then write-in its Pat-Cor™ No. 1. Write the chord symbol above each chord and its Roman numeral below each chord.

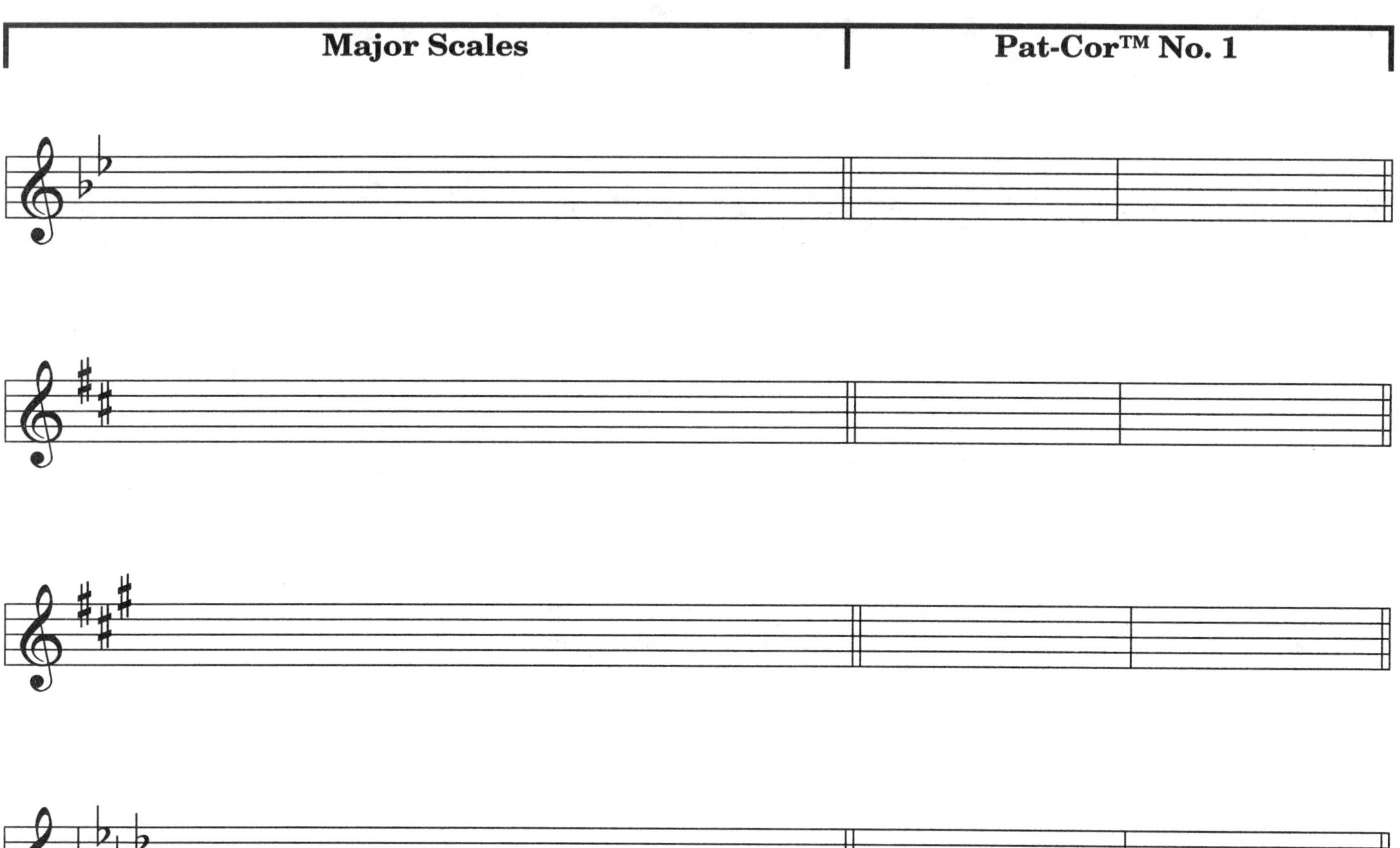

Three Groovin' Mice

TRADITIONAL
Arranged by Richard Bradley

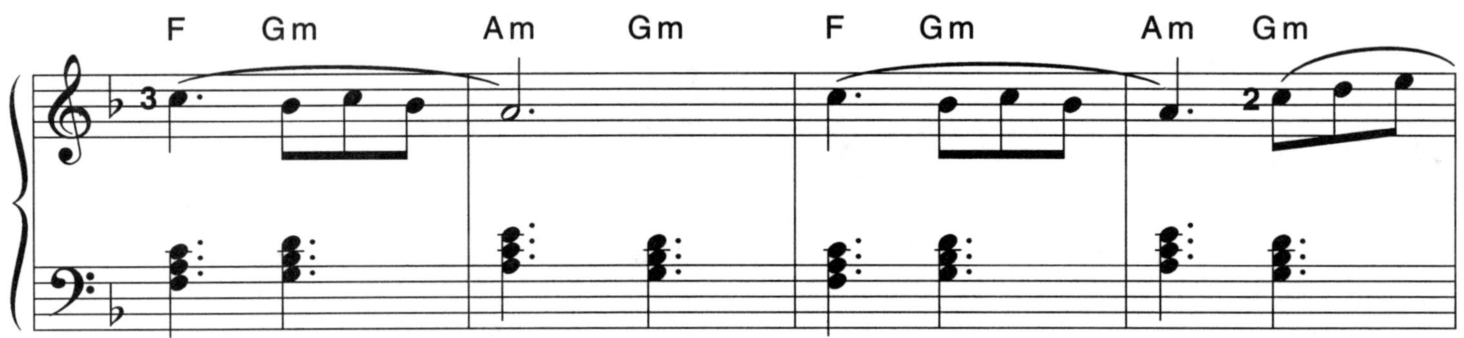

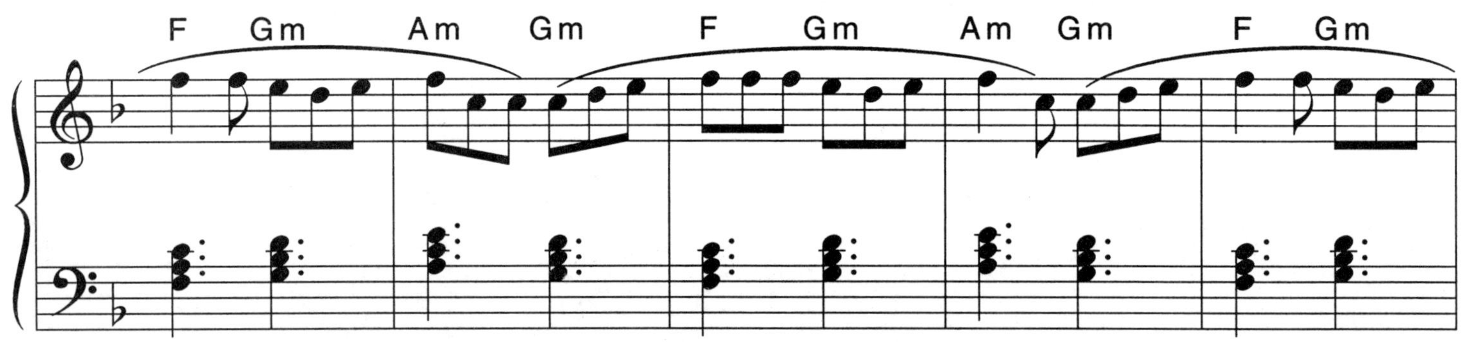

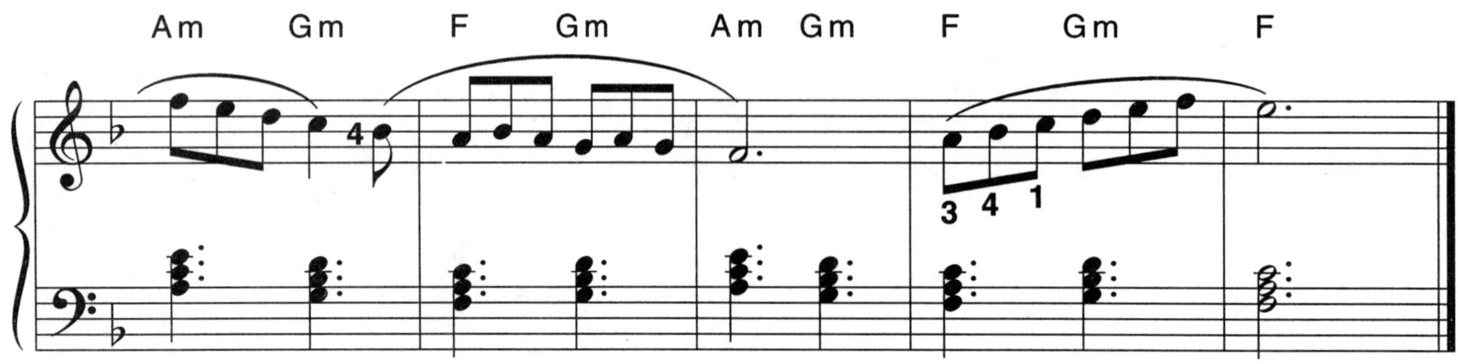

© 1996 BRADLEY PUBLICATIONS
All Rights Reserved

"This Old Man" is in G major. After you play it in G, transpose it to C, then to F.

This Old Man

TRADITIONAL
Arranged by Richard Bradley

© 1996 BRADLEY PUBLICATIONS
All Rights Reserved

German Folk Song

TRADITIONAL
Arranged by Richard Bradley

© 1996 BRADLEY PUBLICATIONS
All Rights Reserved

Modes

Modes are scales consiting of various patterns of whole and half steps. In each key, there are seven modes.

In the key of C, all of the modes will use the notes of the C major scale: From C – C, D – D, E – E, F – F, G – G, A – A, B – B.

Modal improvisation is simply using the notes of a mode to improvise a melody. In the key of C, modal improvisation uses only the white keys on the keyboard. The white keys can be played in any order, any rhythm or any pattern. You can't make a mistake as long as you stay on the white keys.

Pat-Cor™ No. 1 helps us understand what scales and chords to use for an interesting modal improvisation. The right hand will improvise on the notes of the C major scale (all white keys) while the left hand will play the Dm and Em chords.

Music based on modes is very prevalent in "new age music". Listen for the "new age" sound as you play the example below.

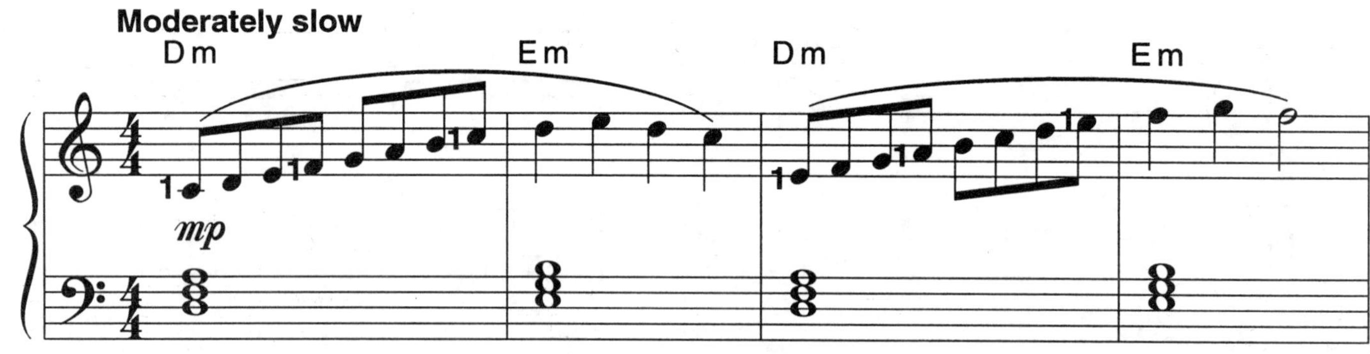

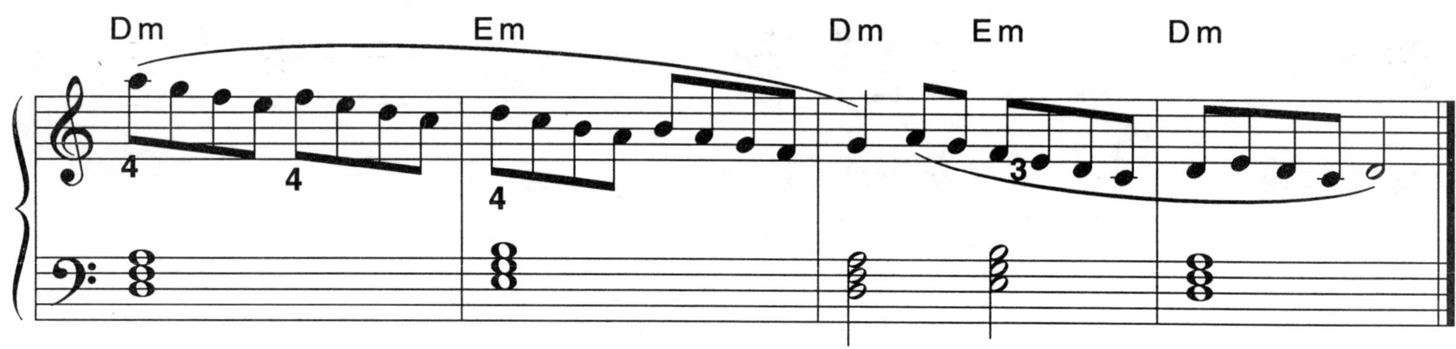

All Modes

By RICHARD BRADLEY

© 1996 BRADLEY PUBLICATIONS
All Rights Reserved

Motives

A **motive** is a short melodic and/or rhythmic pattern. Most pieces are composed of a series of motives.

The same motive can start on any note of the scale. Play the following motive starting on C, G, B and F, then find and play it starting on D, A and E.

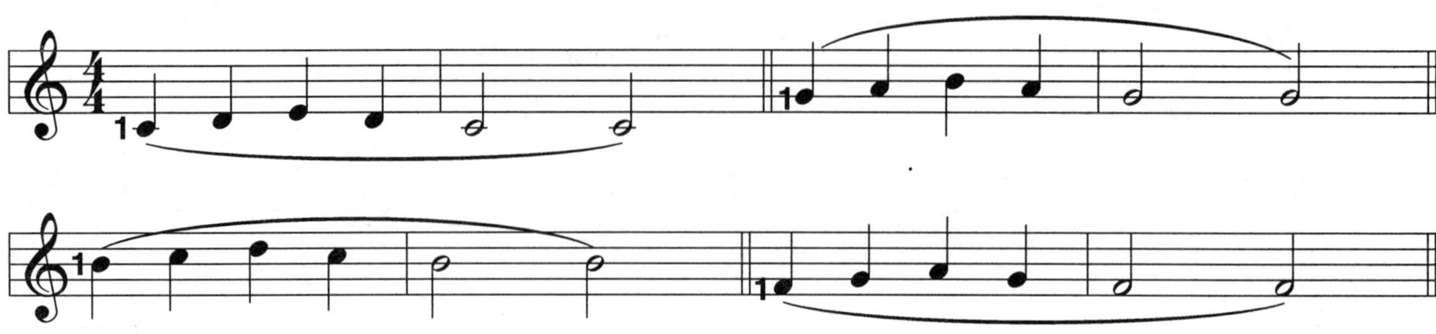

Play the following motive starting on E, A, D and G, then find and play it starting on C, F and B.

Write and play some two measure motives of your own.

Changing the key for a section is a good way to add interest to a piece. In "For Miles", I went up a half step to D♭ using Pat-Cor™ No. 1 in the D♭ scale with E♭m and Fm as the left hand chords.

For Miles

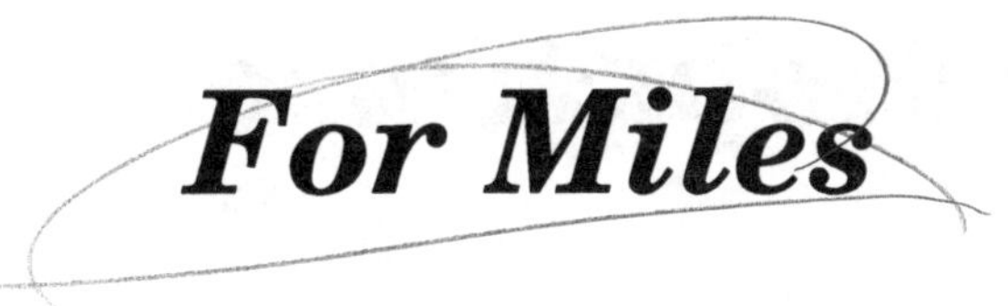

By RICHARD BRADLEY

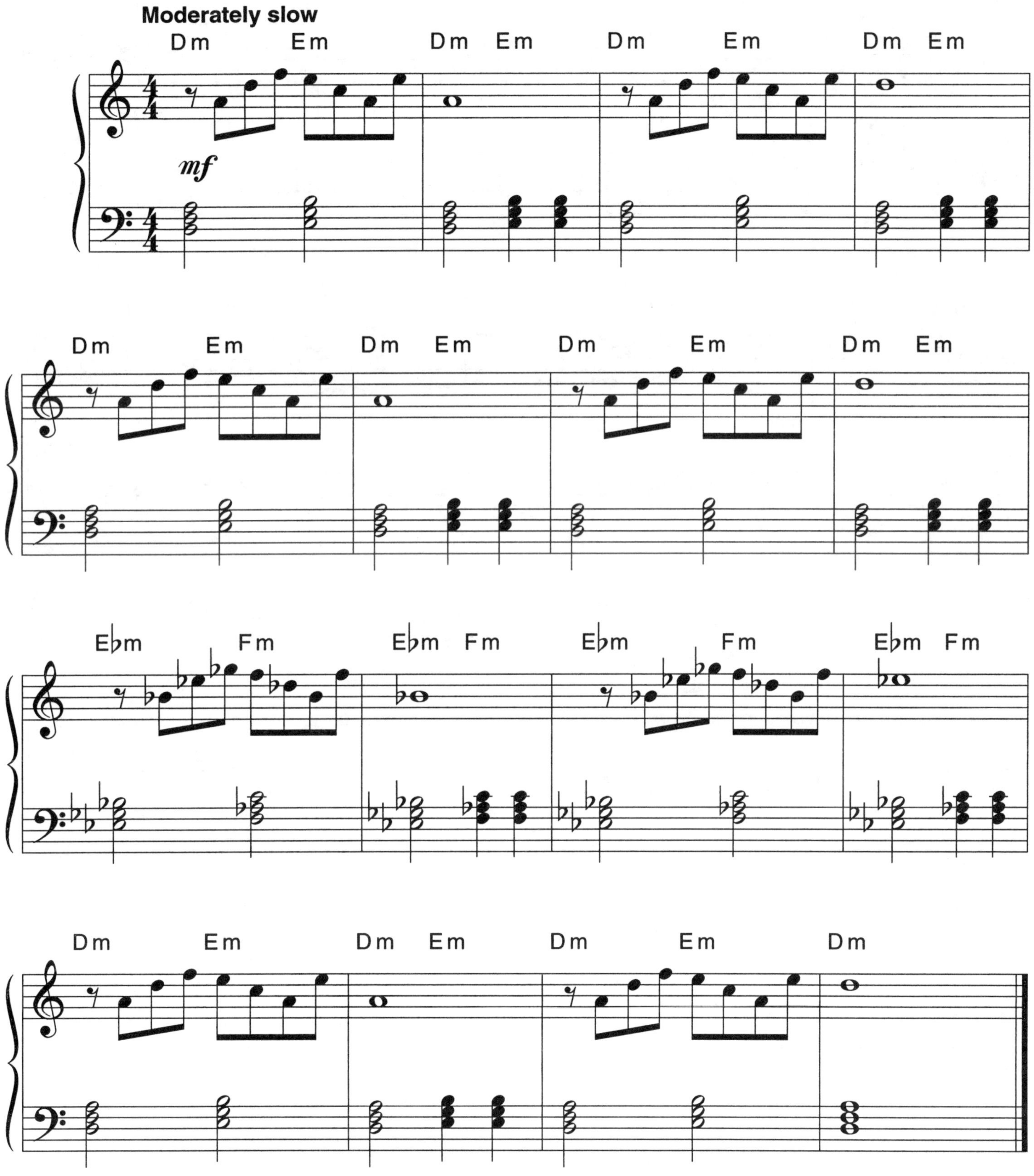
Moderately slow
Dm Em Dm Em Dm Em Dm Em
mf
Dm Em Dm Em Dm Em Dm Em
E♭m Fm E♭m Fm E♭m Fm E♭m Fm
Dm Em Dm Em Dm Em Dm

© 1996 BRADLEY PUBLICATIONS
All Rights Reserved

Play the theme, then improvise on the chords for eight bars. Next, go up a half step to D♭ for eight bars. Go back to the theme in C. Play my written improvisation, then make-up your own motive.

Moondance

Words and Music by
VAN MORRISON
Arranged by Richard Bradley

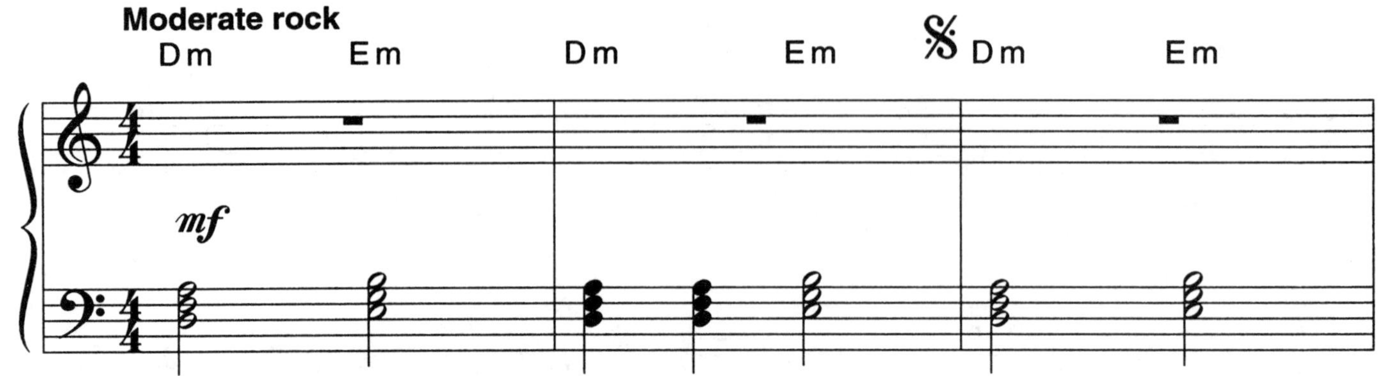

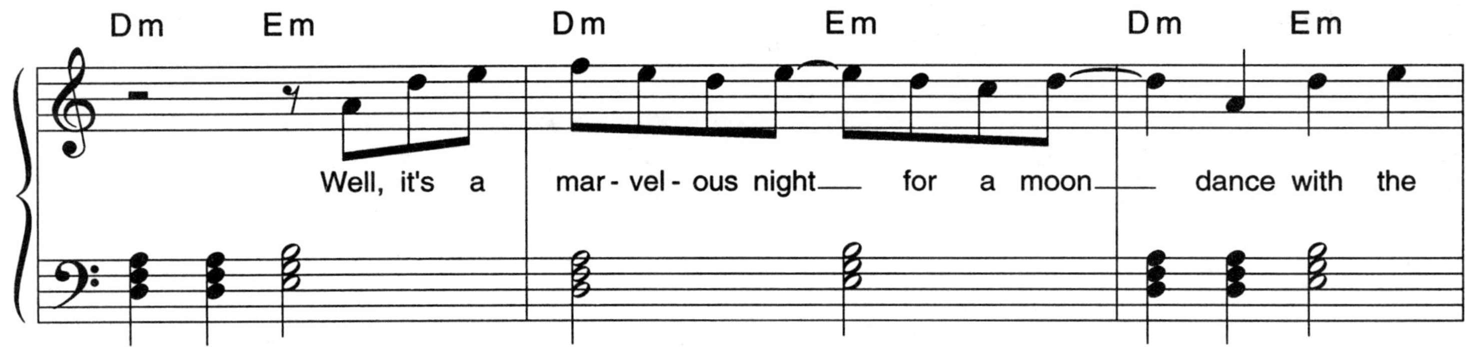

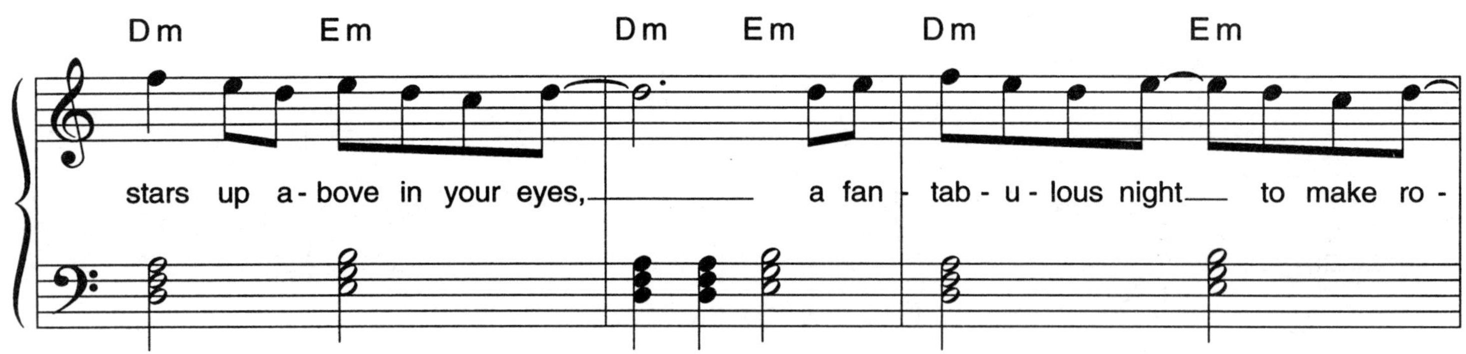

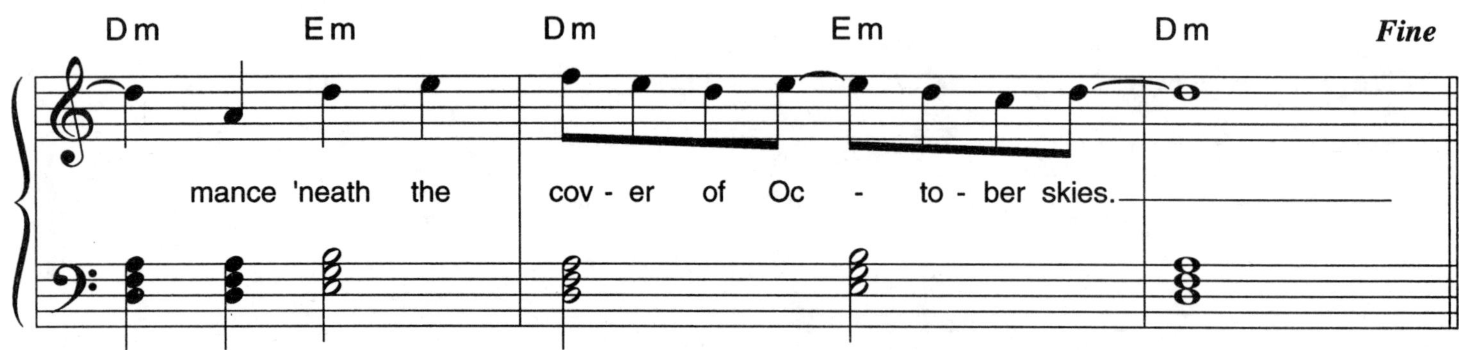

© 1970, 1971 WB MUSIC CORP. and CALEDONIA SOUL MUSIC
This arrangement © 1996 WB MUSIC CORP. and CALEDONIA SOUL MUSIC
All Rights Administered by WB MUSIC CORP.
All Rights Reserved

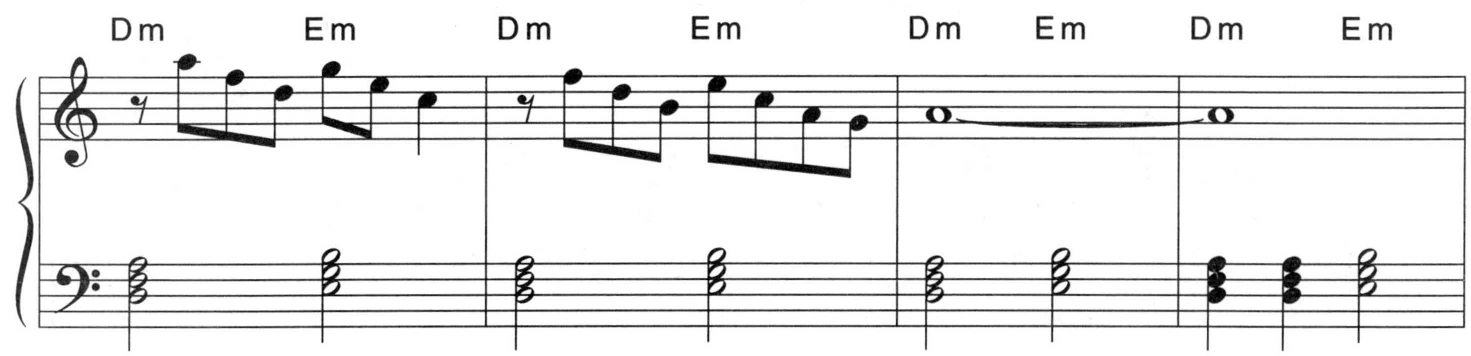
Dm
Em
Dm
Em
Dm
Em
Dm
Em

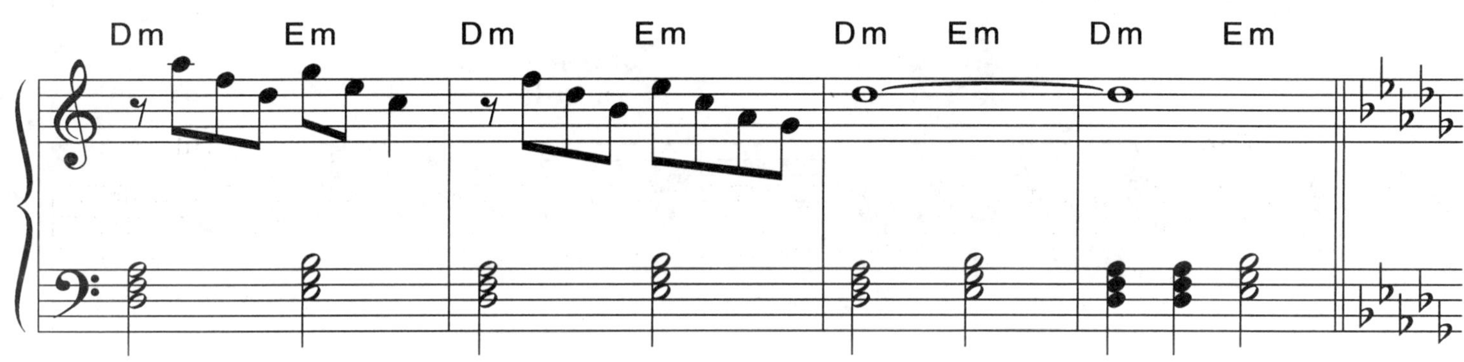
Dm
Em
Dm
Em
Dm
Em
Dm
Em

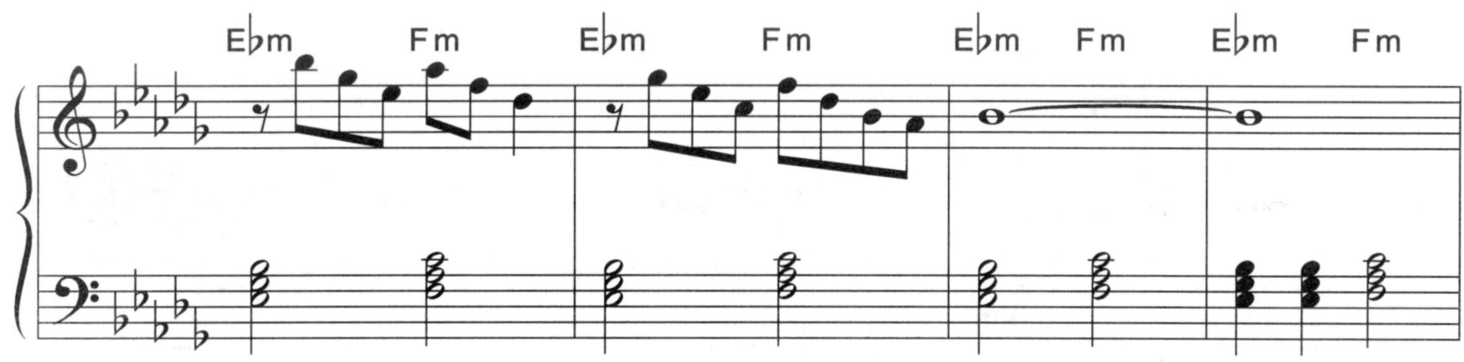
E♭m
Fm
E♭m
Fm
E♭m
Fm
E♭m
Fm

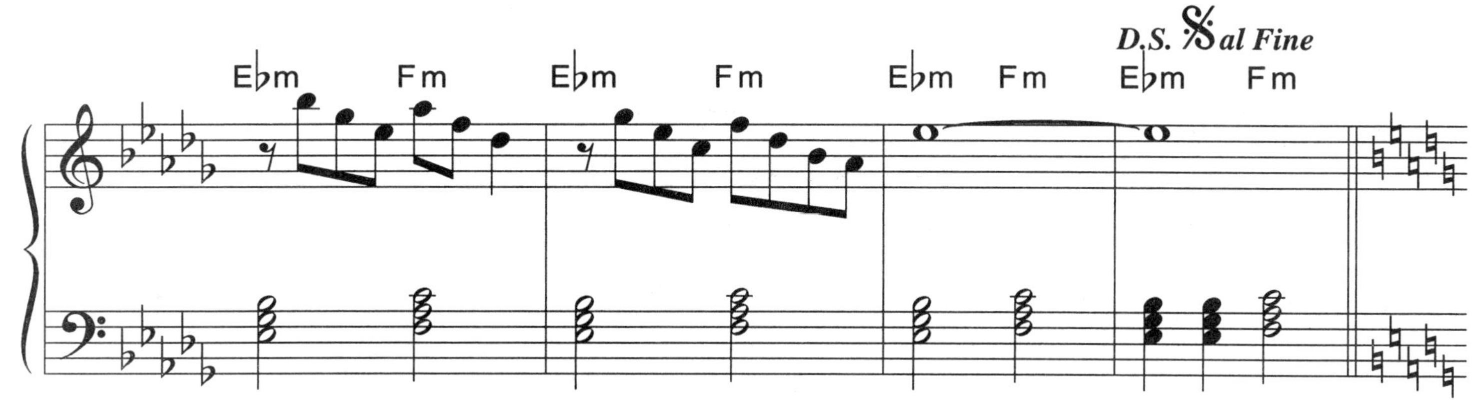
D.S. 𝄋 al Fine
E♭m
Fm
E♭m
Fm
E♭m
Fm
E♭m
Fm

Chord Review

A chord is formed from a root and intervals of a 3rd and a 5th.

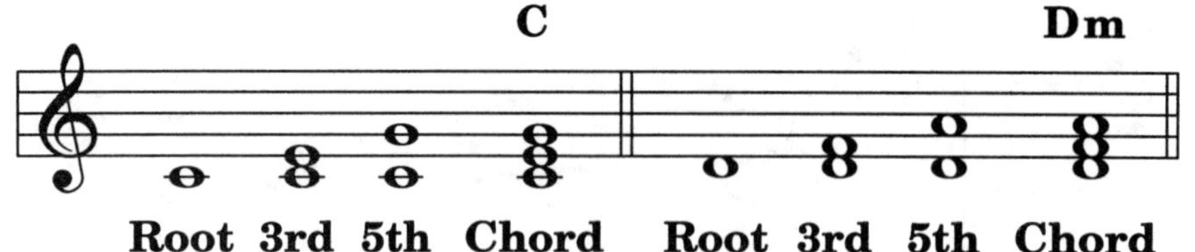

The difference between a major chord and a minor chord is the interval of the 3rd.
A major chord is a major 3rd (4 half steps) and a perfect 5th (7 half steps).
A minor chord is a minor 3rd (3 half steps) and a perfect 5th (7 half steps).

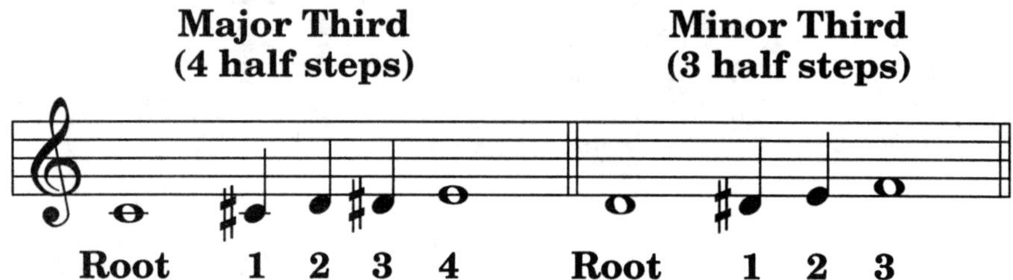

A chord can also be seen as two intervals of a 3rd.
Major chord = Major 3rd and minor 3rd
Minor chord = minor 3rd and Major 3rd

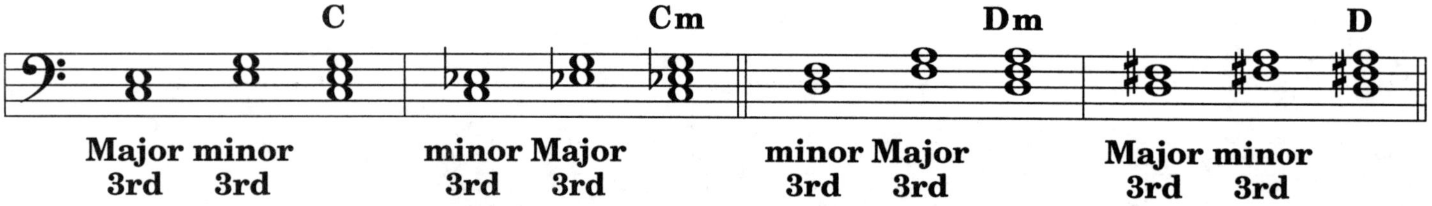

Remember, all chords starting on the root must be:

line – line – line
or
space – space – space

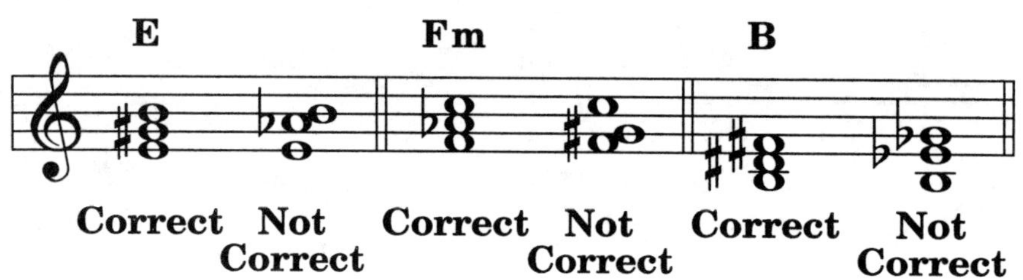

Draw in the notes to complete the following major and minor chords.

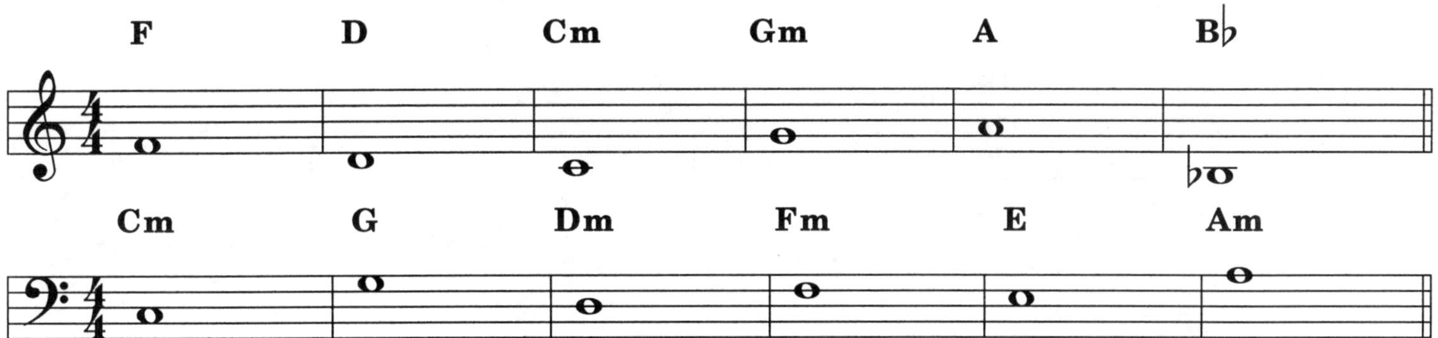

Major to Minor Chords

Play these major chords: C, F and G.
Notice all three are every other white key.
Next, play the major chords followed by the minor chords.

C Cm F Fm G Gm

Play these major chords: D, E and A.
Notice all three are white, black, white.
Next, play the major chords followed by the minor chords.

D Dm E Em A Am

Play these major chords: D♭, E♭ and A♭.
Notice all three are black, white, black.
Next, play the major chords followed by the minor chords.

The chords on the staff below do not have a common look.
Play the major chord followed by the minor chord.
Notice F♯ and G♭ are the same chord with another name. This is referred to as enharmonic.

Simply breaking up the notes of the chords makes an excellent bass line.
Notice the syncopation in the melody.

C
Dm
F
G
Root 3rd 5th
Root 3rd 5th
Root 3rd 5th
Root 3rd 5th

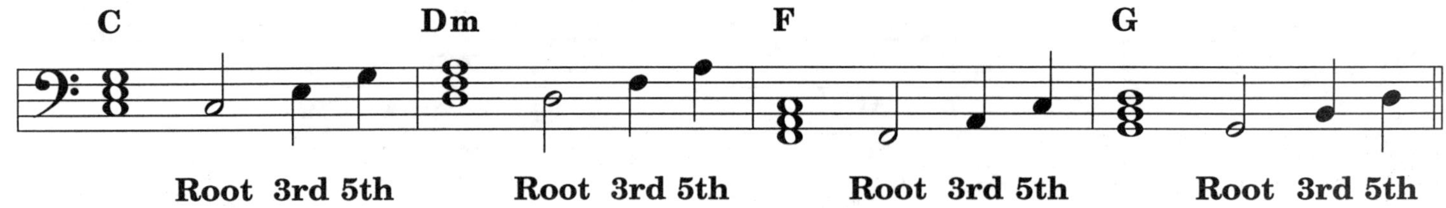

Jamaica Farewell

TRADITIONAL
Arranged by Richard Bradley

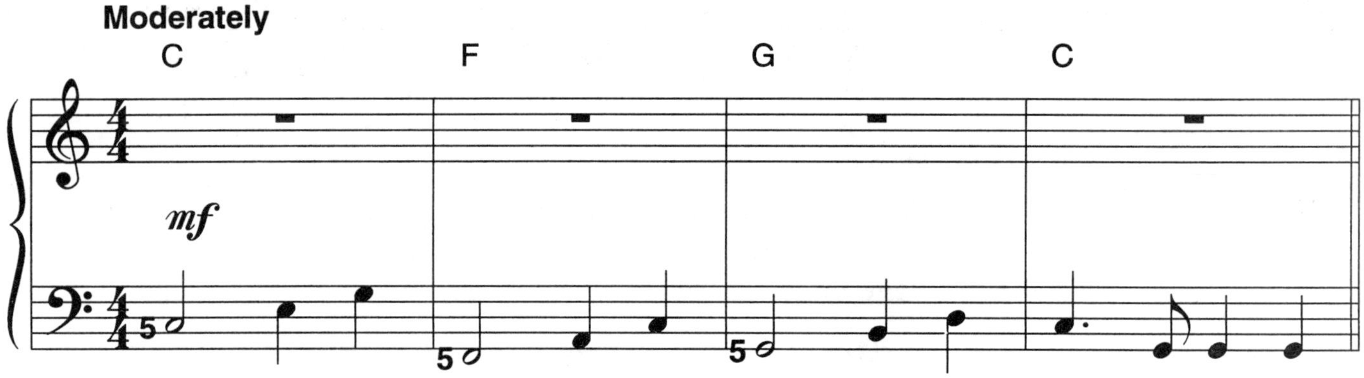
Moderately
C
F
G
C
mf

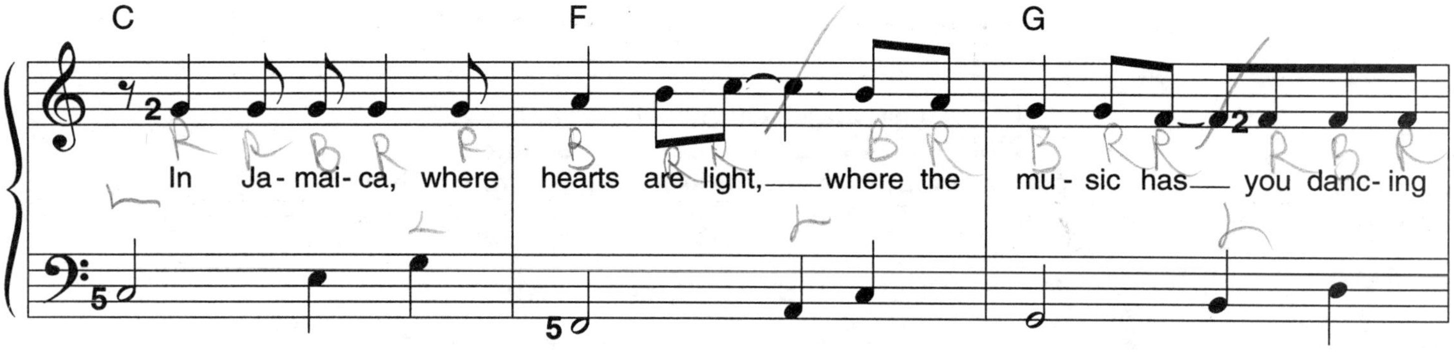
C
F
G
In Ja-mai-ca, where hearts are light, where the mu-sic has you danc-ing

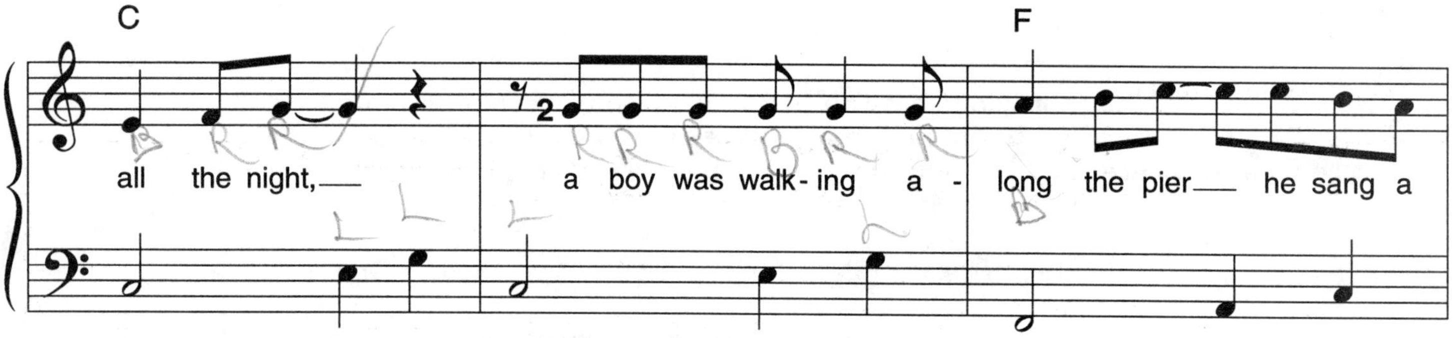
C
F
all the night, a boy was walk-ing a-long the pier he sang a

© 1996 BRADLEY PUBLICATIONS
All Rights Reserved

G
C
4
lit - tle song that I
still can hear. Oh! so
sad am I to

Dm
G
C
1
5
say "good-bye"
I'll come back, no
more will I cry; I

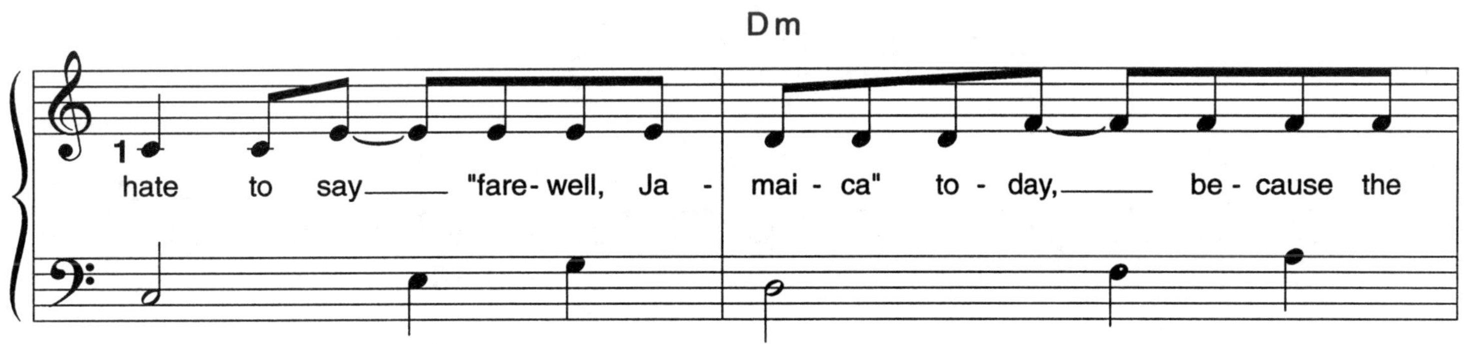
Dm
1
hate to say "fare-well, Ja -
mai - ca" to - day, be - cause the

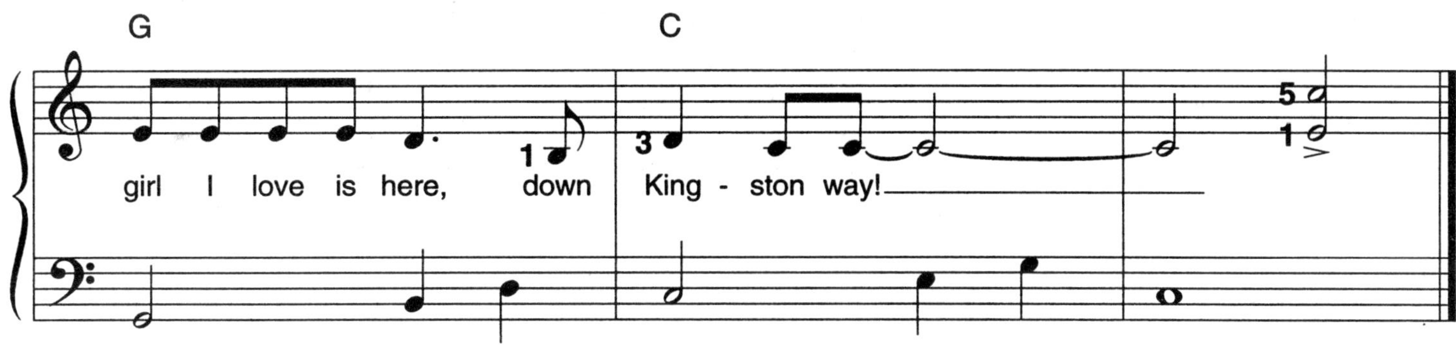
G
C
1
3
5
1
girl I love is here, down
King - ston way!

La Cucaracha

TRADITIONAL
MEXICAN FOLK SONG
Arranged by Richard Bradley

© 1996 BRADLEY PUBLICATIONS
All Rights Reserved

D
G
D
G

The 12 Bar Blues

The blues uses a twelve bar chord progression.
The basic blues uses the I, IV and V chords of the scale.
In the key of C, it is:

4 bars of	**I**	**C**
2 bars of	**IV**	**F**
2 bars of	**I**	**C**
1 bar of	**V**	**G**
1 bar of	**IV**	**F**
2 bars of	**I**	**C**

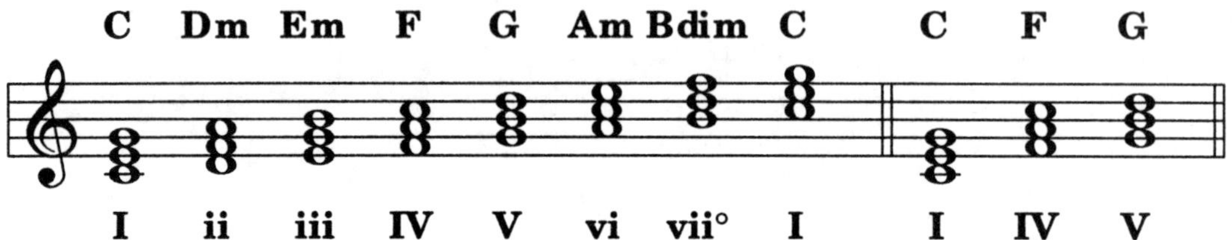

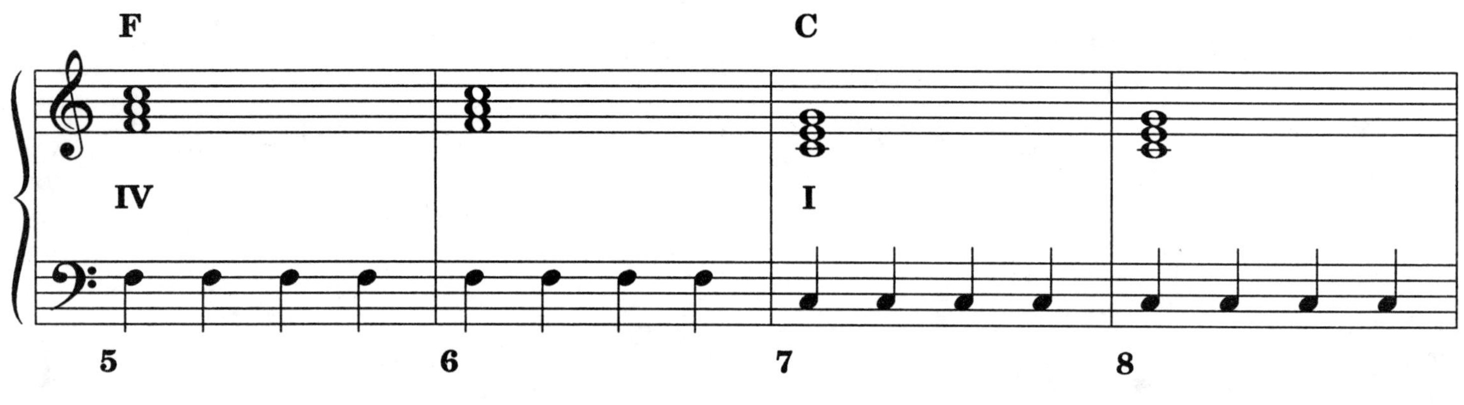

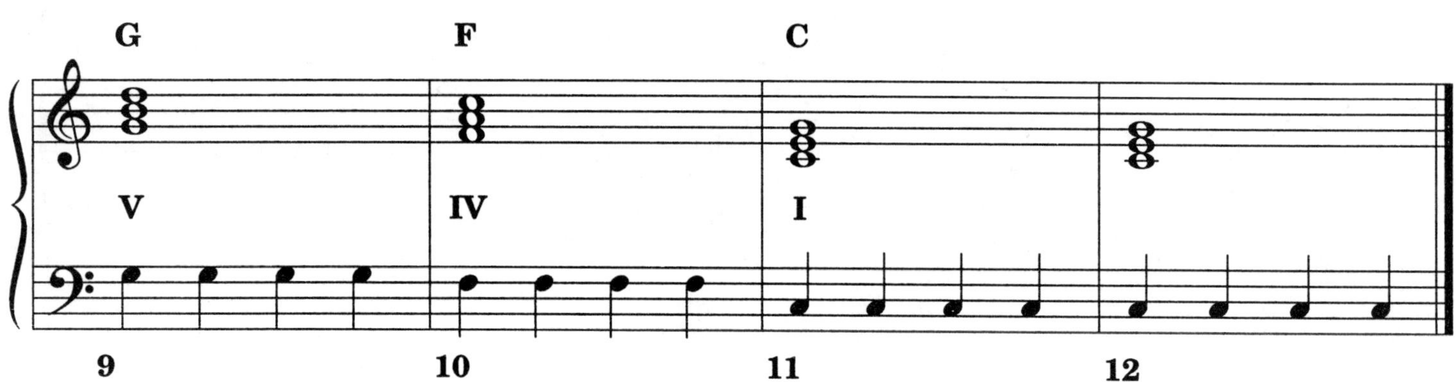

In 1912, W. C. Handy's "Memphis Blues" became the first blues to be published, but a substantial part of the blues tradition is improvising.

Ma Rainey, Bessie Smith and Huddie Ledbetter were among the early exponents of the blues. Today, the blues is more popular than ever. Blues clubs are popping up all over the world. There are The House Of Blues, and B. B. King's and Chicago Blues among scores of others. There are also many styles of blues: New Orleans sound, a Chicago style and Memphis sound.

The blues is an important part of playing any jazz, rock, funk or popular style of music. It is necessary not only to memorize the twelve bar progression, but to **hear when the chord changes occur**. The blues is the natural second step to learning improvisation after modal improvisation, since only three chords are involved.

Play the example below, and sing the repeated melody notes: CCCC, CCCC, CCCC, CCCC, FFFF, etc. Next, without playing the right hand notes, sing them again as you accompany yourself with the left hand chords.

The next few examples may not be the most exciting pieces you have played, but they will help develop your improvising skills and further develop your ear.

The following piece simply uses the notes of the chord as a right hand improvisation. Play "12 Bar Blues", then make-up other several other right hand parts. A motive built on C, F and G is another good way to improvise.

12 Bar Blues

By RICHARD BRADLEY

© 1996 BRADLEY PUBLICATIONS
All Rights Reserved

We have already learned that breaking up the notes of a chord creates a bass line pattern. This can be done in various ways. Play the twelve bar example below as written. Notice the right hand rhythm of each line is the same (a four measure rhythm pattern). Next change the chords to other beats. Try these two measure rhythm patterns and make-up some of your own.

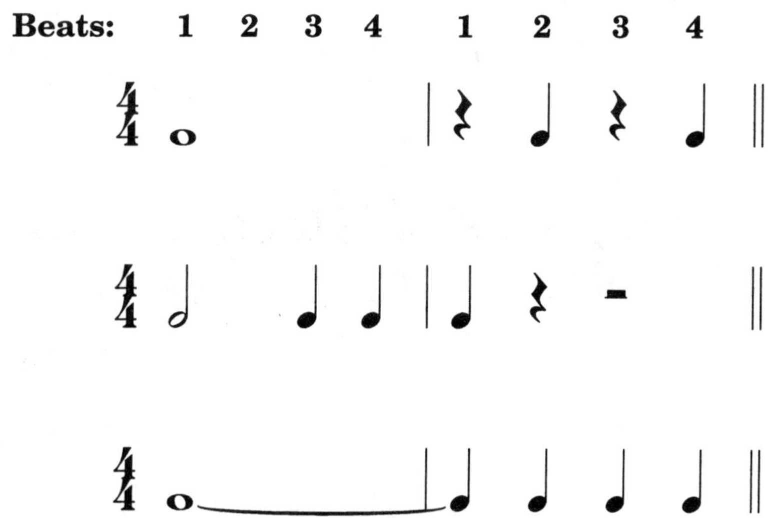

Moderately slow

C
I
mf
1 2 3 4

F IV
C I
5 6 7 8

G V
F IV
C I
9 10 11 12

The following bass line pattern is a broken chord with both the minor and major 3rd.

Minor To Major Blues

By RICHARD BRADLEY

Moderately

C

f

F C

G F C

© 1996 BRADLEY PUBLICATIONS
All Rights Reserved

The **blue note** is a minor third played against a major chord.
It is often played as a grace note sliding into the major third.

A **passing tone** is a note between two chord tones. It makes a good bass line.

Blue Note Blues

By RICHARD BRADLEY

Moderately slow

C

mf

5 3

1 2 3 4

F C

5 6 7 8

G F C

9 10 11 12

© 1996 BRADLEY PUBLICATIONS
All Rights Reserved

A **walking bass** pattern simulates a bass player.
You play the note name of the chord followed by the next three descending notes of the scale.

Walking Bass Blues

By RICHARD BRADLEY

Moderately slow

C

mf

1 2 3 4

F C

5 6 7 8

G F C

9 10 11 12

© 1996 BRADLEY PUBLICATIONS
All Rights Reserved

Notice the left hand walking bass as your play "L.A. Blues". The right hand plays a chord on the first and fourth beat of each measure. Experiment playing each of the right hand rhythm patterns in the following example above the "L.A. Blues" walking bass. Make-up some of your own.

1
2
3
4
1 2 3 4 1 2 3 4
5
6
7
8
1 2 & 3 4 1 & 2 & 3–4

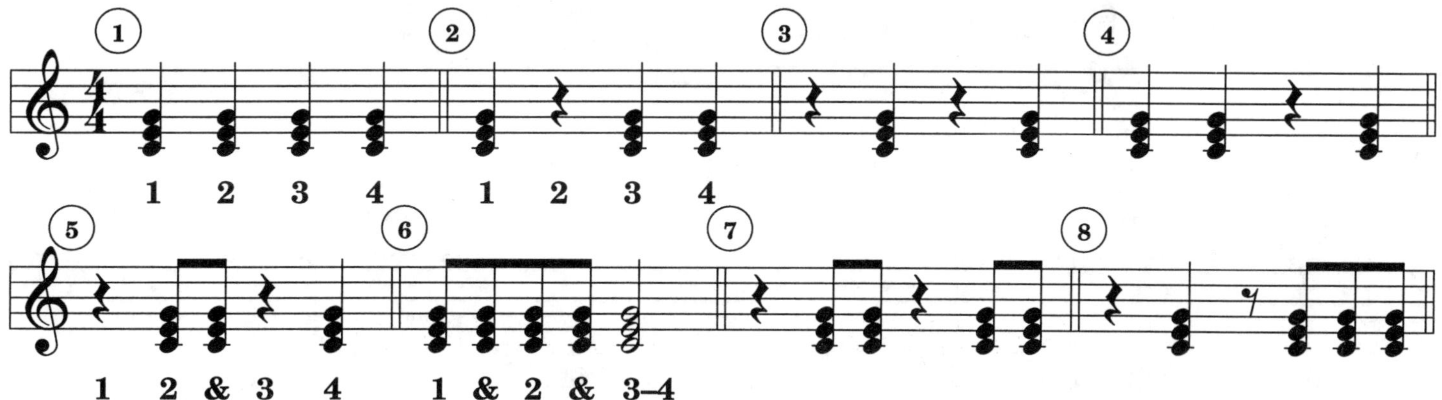

L.A. Blues

By RICHARD BRADLEY

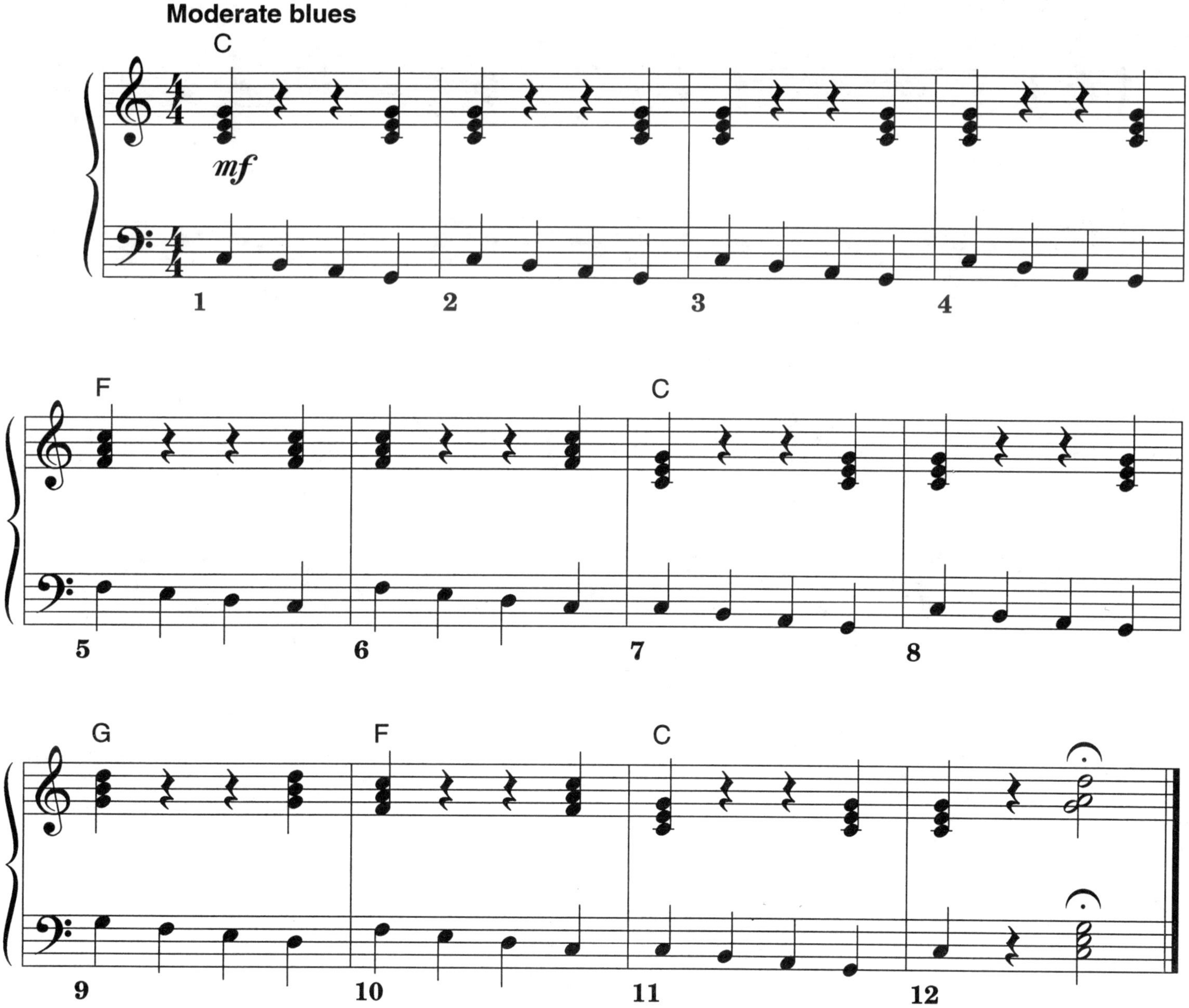

Moderate blues
C
mf
1
2
3
4
F
C
5
6
7
8
G
F
C
9
10
11
12

© 1996 BRADLEY PUBLICATIONS
All Rights Reserved

The interval of a sixth added to each major chord creates a richer sound. This four note chord is called a sixth and is written with the chord letter name followed by the number 6.

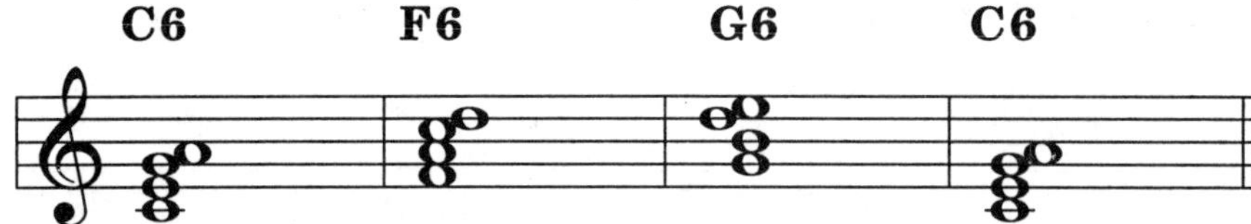

The intervals of a fifth and sixth creates a moving boogie rhythm.

Blues At Six

By RICHARD BRADLEY

Steady

C6 *mf* 1 2 3 4

F6 C6 5 6 7 8

G6 F6 C6 *rit.* 9 10 11 12

© 1996 BRADLEY PUBLICATIONS
All Rights Reserved

Another common boogie pattern uses the sixth in the bass pattern:

Root – 3rd – 5th – 6th – Octave – 6th – 5th – 3rd

Boogie Sticks

Moderate boogie

By RICHARD BRADLEY

C6

mf

F6 C6

G6 F6 C6

© 1996 BRADLEY PUBLICATIONS
All Rights Reserved

The seventh chord, another four note chord, has a "bluesy" sound.
The seventh note is a half step above the sixth. It is added to the major chord.
The seventh chord is written with the letter name followed by the number 7.

The seventh can also be found as one whole step below the root.
The seventh will change the I (C) and IV (F) chords in the walking bass we have been using.

Good Evening Friends Blues

By RICHARD BRADLEY

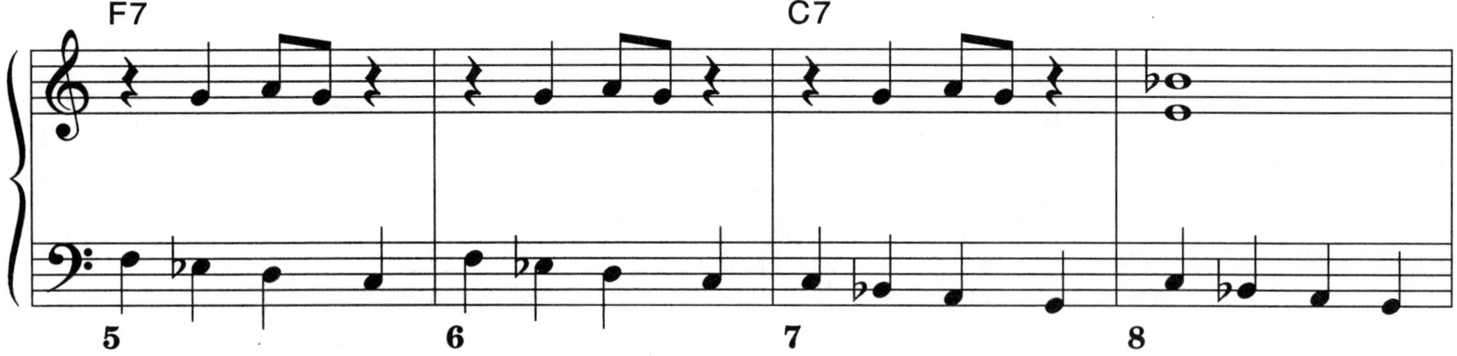

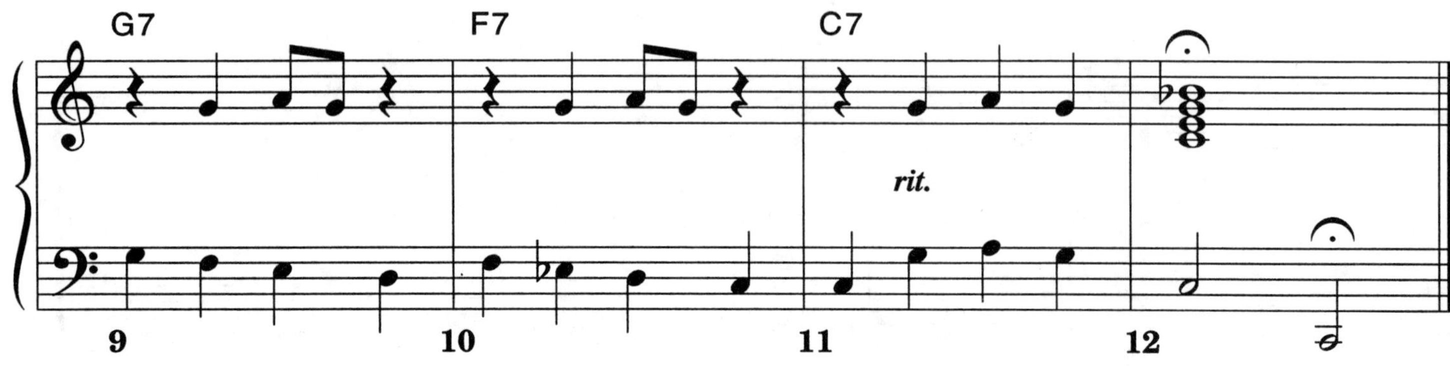

© 1996 BRADLEY PUBLICATIONS
All Rights Reserved

Review

An octave is the distance between two notes of the same letter name, either up or down on the keyboard: C – C, F – F, D – D, etc. On the staff, octaves are always space to line or line to space.

The seventh (minor seventh) is the note one whole step or two half steps below the octave: C – B♭, G – F, D – C, etc. On the staff, the notes of a seventh are always both on lines or both on spaces.

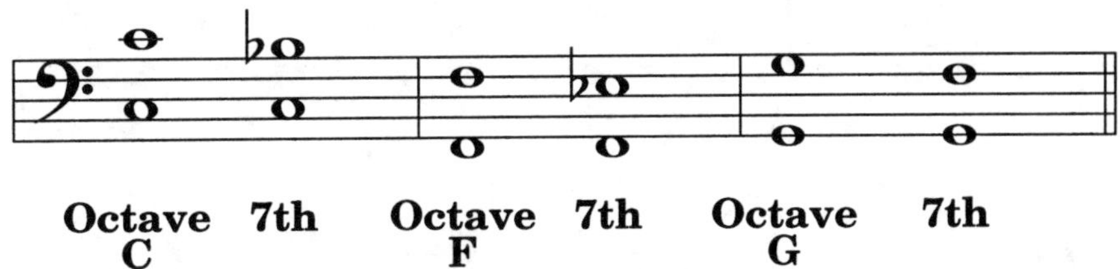

The interval of a seventh can be added to any major chord.
The chord becomes C7, E7, F7, etc.

The interval of a seventh can also be added to any minor chord.
The chord becomes Cm7, Em7, Fm7, etc.

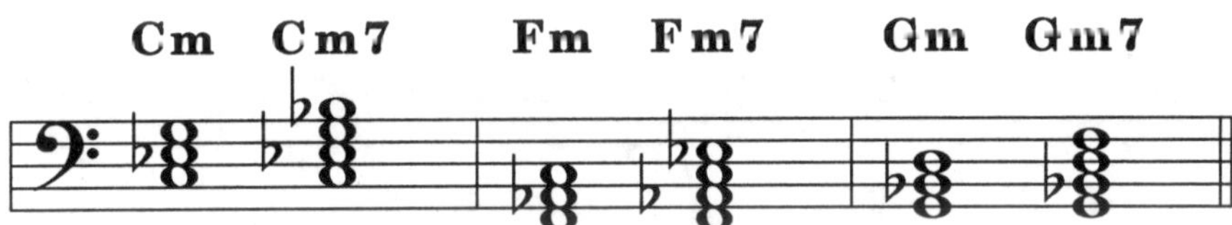

Draw in the notes to complete all of the major, 7th, minor and m7 chords below, then play them.

Play the major, then the minor chords for each key.
Do you hear the difference?

Play the 7th and m7 for easch key.
Do you hear the difference?

D D7 Dm Dm7 B♭ B♭7 B♭m B♭m7 E E7 Em Em7 A A7 Am Am7

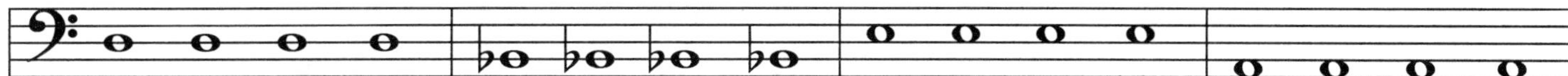

E♭ E♭7 E♭m E♭m7 B B7 Bm Bm7 A♭ A♭7 A♭m A♭m7 D♭ D♭7 D♭m D♭m7

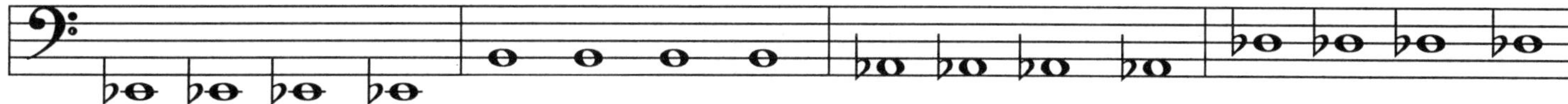

The blues is a form of music where all of the chords can be played as seventh chords: C = C7, F = F7, G = G7, etc.

Instead of playing a full four note seventh chord, which can be too deep and muddy sounding, just the interval of the seventh is often used. Jazz musicians refer to this as **shell voicing**. Like the outside of the shell of an egg, only the outside of the chord is played.

Preservation Hall Parade

By RICHARD BRADLEY

Slow march

C7

1 2 3 4

F7 C7

5 6 7 8

G7 F7 C7

9 10 11 12

© 1996 BRADLEY PUBLICATIONS
All Rights Reserved

You can combine sixth and seventh chords. The bass pattern below is based on a sixth chord, while the right hand plays some of the notes of the seventh chords. As its title indicates, "Pick Up Blues" starts with three pick up notes.

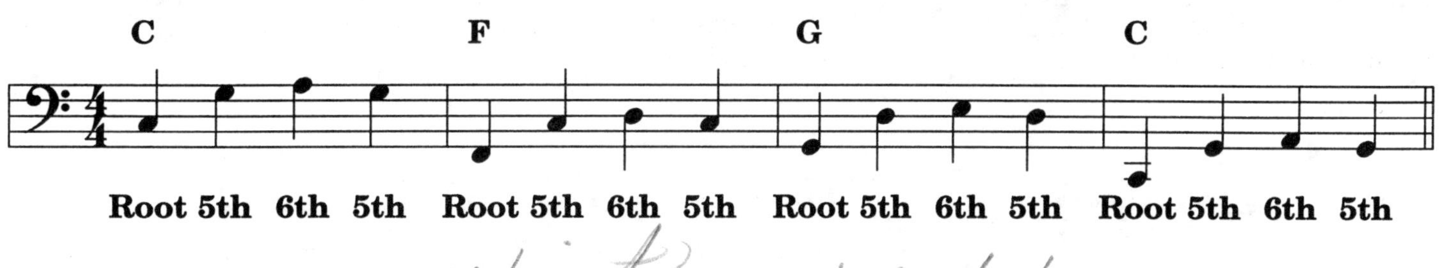

vamp – ostinato – repeated pattern

Pick Up Blues

By RICHARD BRADLEY

Slow blues

C6

mp

1 2 3 4

F7 C6

5 6 7 8

G7 F♯7 F7 C

9 10 11 12

© 1996 BRADLEY PUBLICATIONS
All Rights Reserved

You can create a very "bluesy" sound by changing two notes of the C major scale: flat 3rd (blue note) and flat 7th.

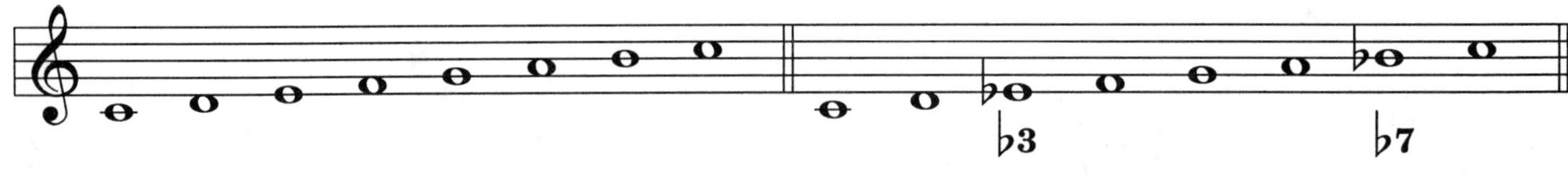

Flat Feet Blues

By RICHARD BRADLEY

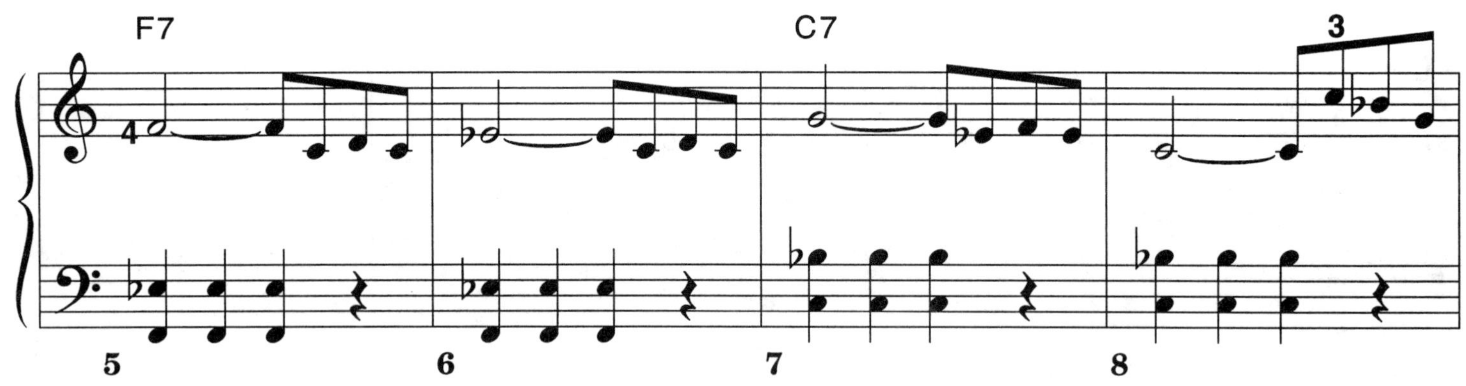

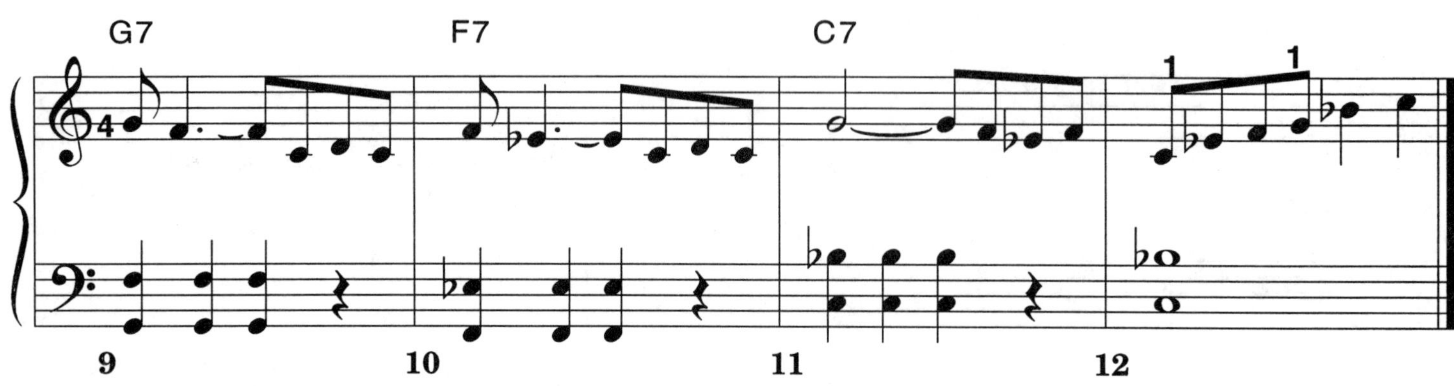

© 1996 BRADLEY PUBLICATIONS
All Rights Reserved

Melodic Improvisation

The trick to **melodic improvisation** is knowing which notes to play.
To begin, play only these three notes. They are part of the C major blues scale.

The next step is knowing when to play them.
Here are three different two measure motives (or riffs as some jazz musicians call them):

1. Play the first rhythm using only one note: C.
2. Play the first rhythm using two notes in any order: C and E♭.
3. Play the first rhythm using all three notes in any order: C, E♭ and F.
4. Follow the same steps with rhythm two, then rhythm three.
5. Play the following walking bass pattern under all three motives using all three notes.

Now, improvise using only these three notes:

Use these two measure motives:

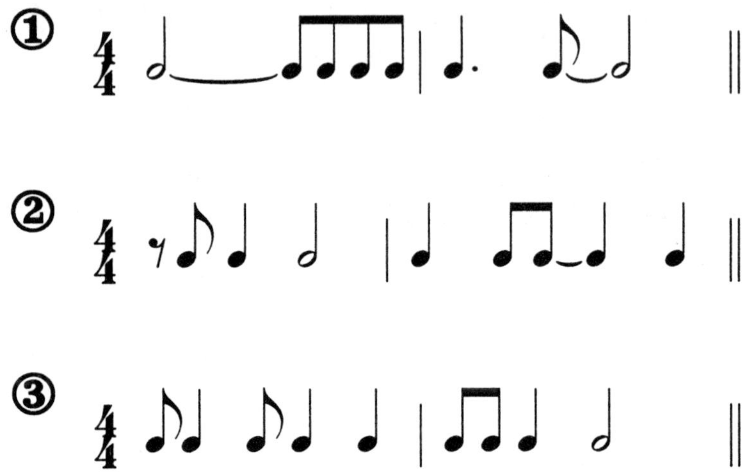

1. Play the first rhythm using only one note: C.
2. Play the first rhythm using two notes in any order: C and B♭.
3. Play the first rhythm using all three notes in any order: C, B♭ and G.
4. Follow the same steps with rhythm two, then rhythm three.
5. Play the following bass line under all three motives or riffs using all three notes. Play slow enough to keep a steady rhythm.

The notes of the major chord plus the sixth and seventh produce one of the most recognized boogie patterns.

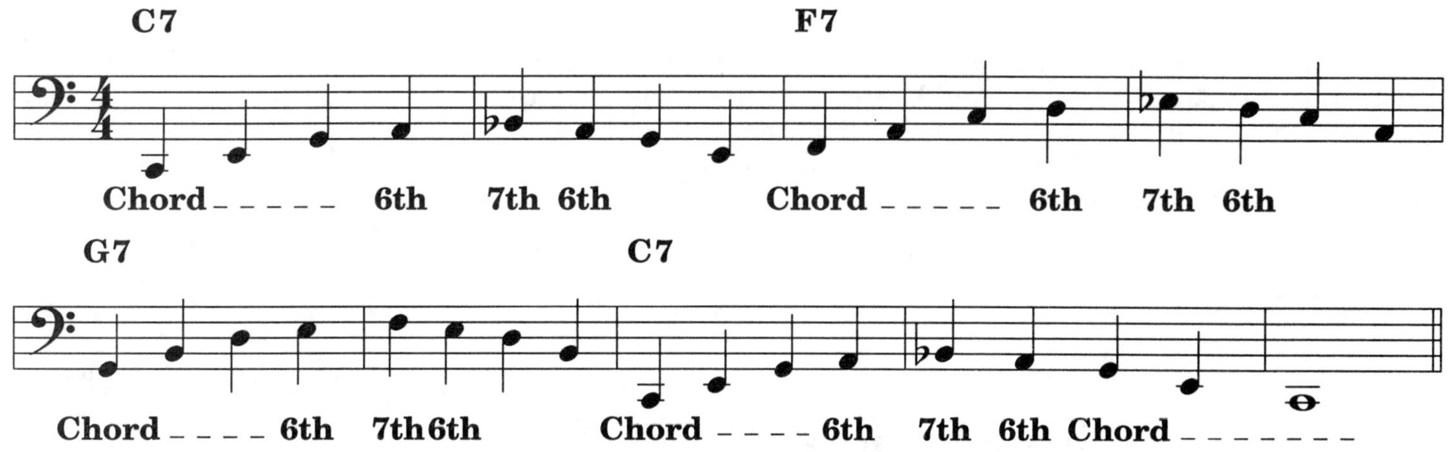

Improvise your right hand.
Use any of the riffs on pages 53 and 54, or make-up your own.
Write your favorite in the treble clef below.

C7

1 2 3 4

F7 C7

5 6 7 8

G6 F6 C7

9 10 11 12

Circle Of Chords

We are familiar and comfortable playing the twelve bar blues in C. We also know it uses the I, IV and V chords of the C major scale. Chords can also progress around a circle spaced by fourths. Look at the circle to the right. Notice the V and IV chords are neighbors of the I chord (on each side of it).

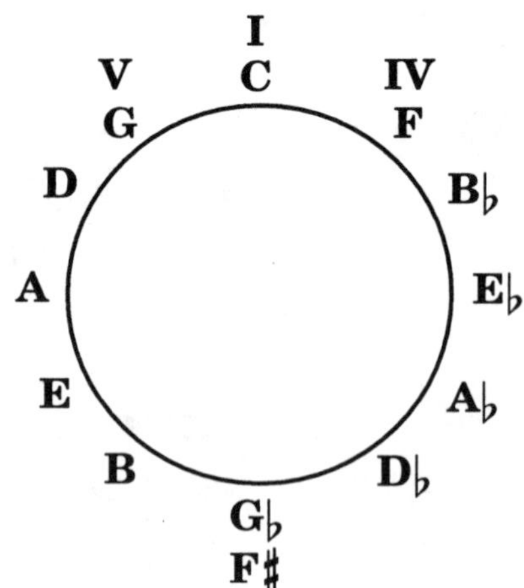

Playing The Blues In F

Playing the blues in F still uses the I, IV and V chord; this time from the F major scale.

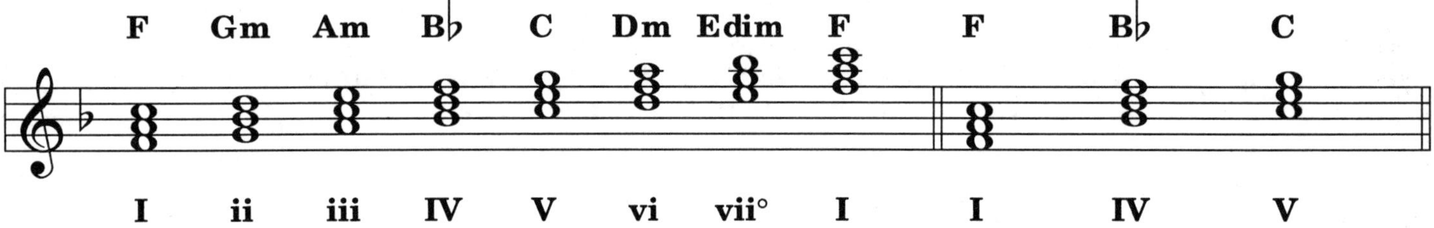

Look at the circle of chords to the right. Notice the V and IV chords are still neighbors of the I chord (still on each side of it).

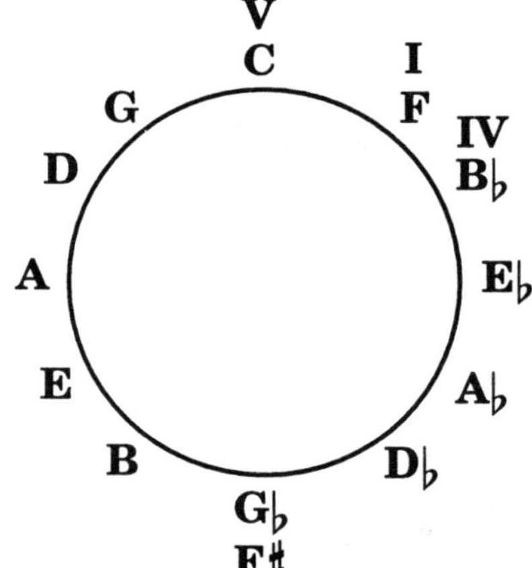

Pick one of your favorite blues in C and play it in F.

Blues In F

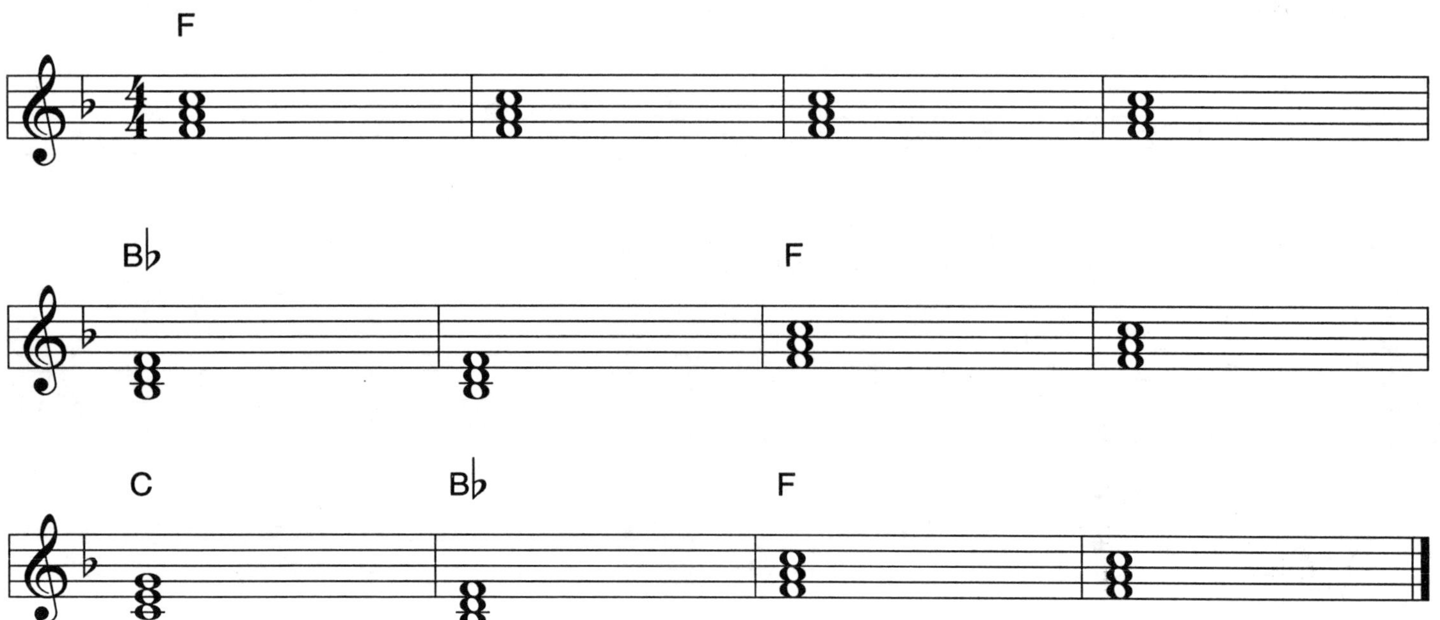

Boogie Board Boogie

By RICHARD BRADLEY

* a G7 over a F7 chord creates a F13 ♯11

© 1996 BRADLEY PUBLICATIONS
All Rights Reserved

Dotted Eighth, Sixteenth Note Rhythm

A dotted eight note is equal to three sixteenth notes.
The following exercises will help develop the feel for the dotted eighth, sixteenth rhythm.
Look at the following examples. They are all three beats followed by one beat.
They can be counted in the following ways:

1 2 3 – 4
1 & 2 – & – 3 & 4 – &
1 e & – a – 2 e & – a – 3 e & – a – 4 e & – a

Bouncy Boogie Bass

This bouncy boogie bass line is a traditional boogie sound.
After you are comfortable playing it, add a right hand chord.
Experiment playing the chord on various beats.

Echo Boogie

By RICHARD BRADLEY

© 1996 BRADLEY PUBLICATIONS
All Rights Reserved

Chord Inversions

A chord is in root position when the name of the chord (its root) is the bottom note. Chords can be **inverted.** To go from the root position to the first inversion, you bring the bottom note to the top. To go from the first inversion to the second inversion, you again bring the bottom note to the top.

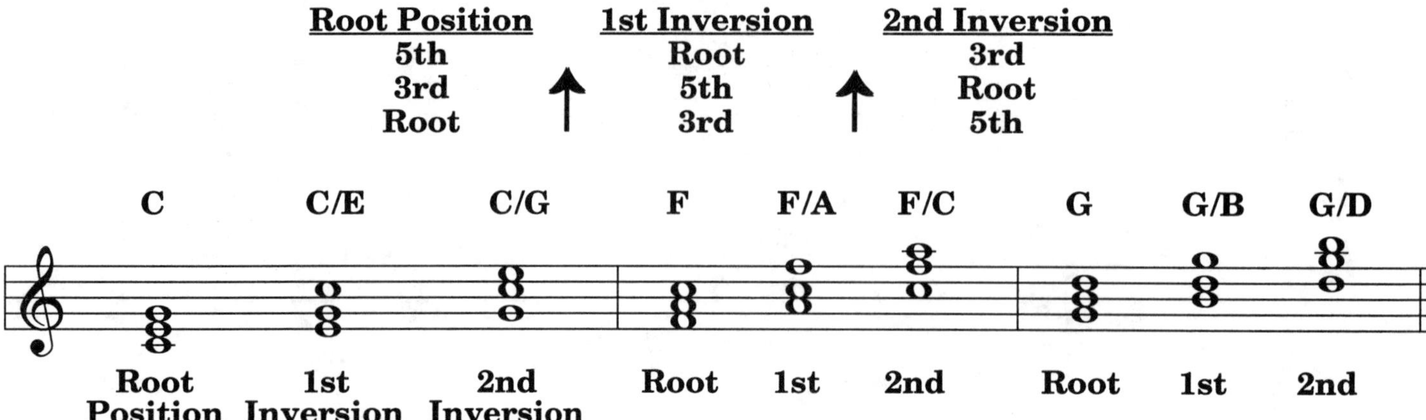

Write root, 1st or 2nd under each chord below.
Root Position: Root is on the bottom. Notes must be all on lines or all on spaces.
1st Inversion: Root is on the top of the chord.
2nd Inversion: Root is in the middle of the chord.

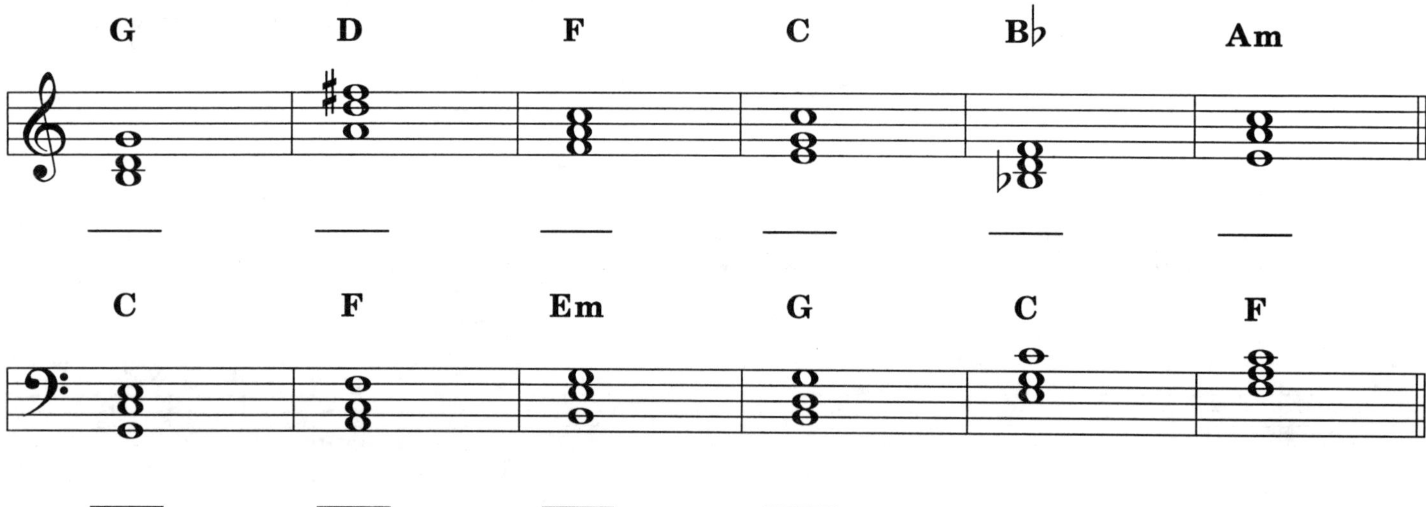

First Inversion Chords On The C Major Scale:

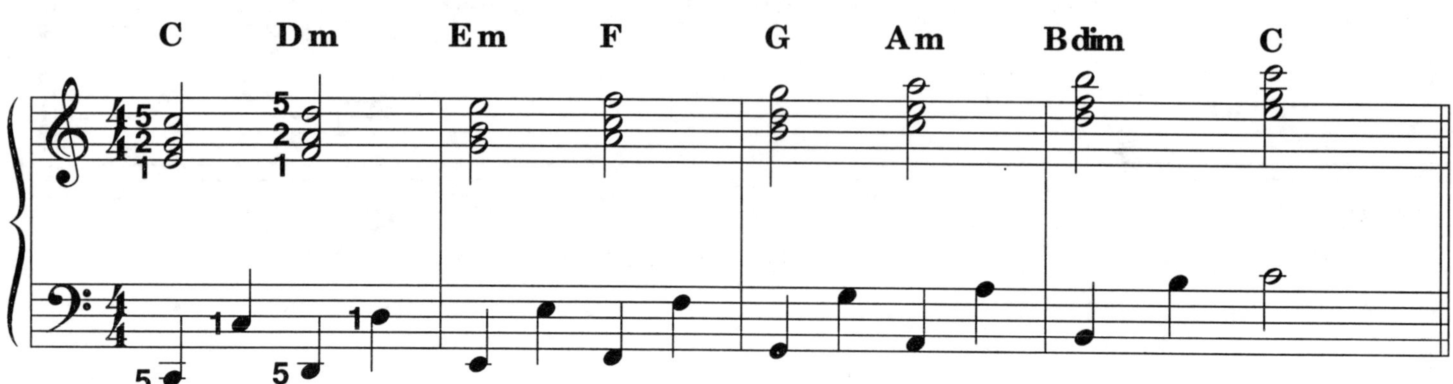

The big band and Bette Midler hit "In The Mood" was based on the blues tune "Tar Paper Stomp". Notice the composer stayed with the "G" chord for both bars nine and ten to continue the pattern.

Tar Paper Stomp

By WINGY MANONE
Arranged by Richard Bradley

Moderately

C

1 2 5 1

1st Inversion

mf

1

1 2 3 4

F

1 3

Root position

C

1 2 5

1st Inversion

5 6 7 8

G

1

Root position

C F C

5
2
1

9 10 11 12

© 1996 BRADLEY PUBLICATIONS
All Rights Reserved

The following chords are all in the first inversion (root on top).
Play this locking your fingers in place.
Can you complete the tune?

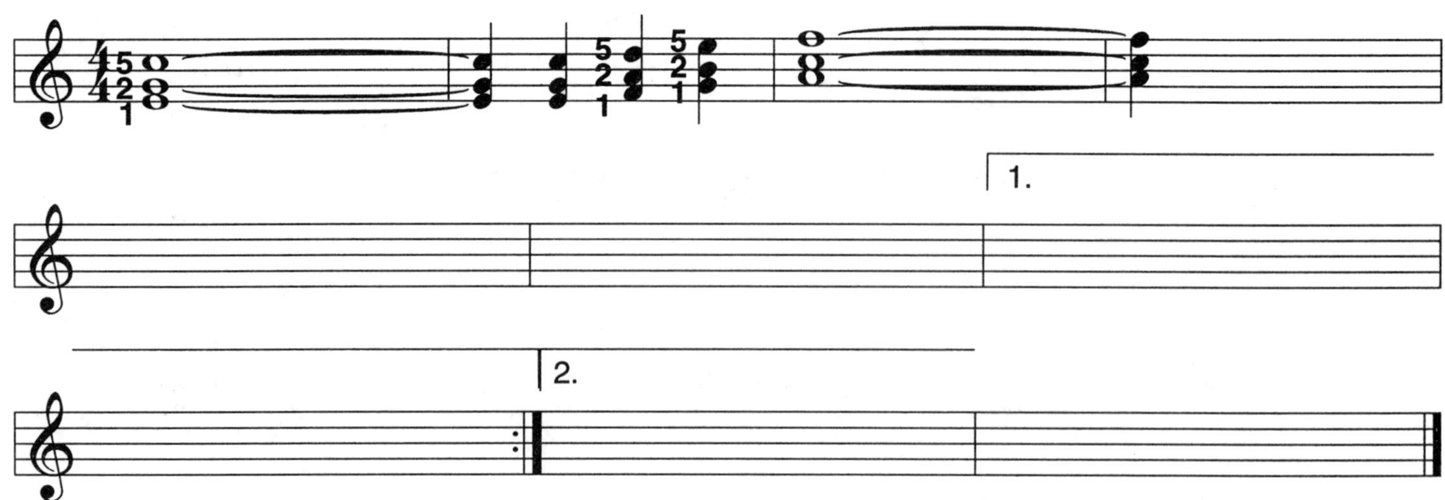

Draw a chord in the first inversion under each melody note below.
Name each chord, then play the completed song.

Down By The Station

Notice the big skip to the G chord in measure three of "Ach, Du Lieber Augustine" below.
Look at the next page and see how the G chord in its first inversion is easier. It sounds better too.

Ach, Du Lieber Augustine

GERMAN FOLK TUNE

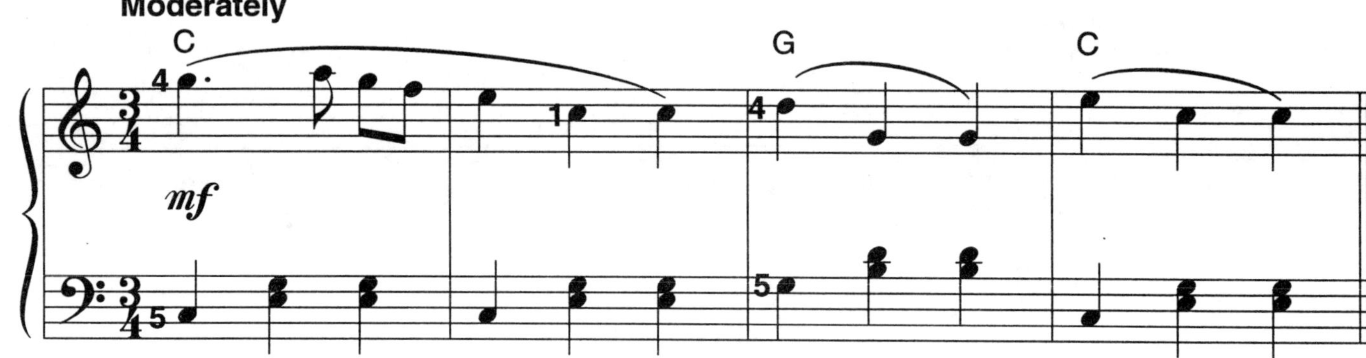

Ach, Du Lieber Augustine

GERMAN FOLK SONG
Arranged by Richard Bradley

© 1996 BRADLEY PUBLICATIONS
All Rights Reserved

An **ostinato** is a melodic and/or rhythmic pattern that is persistant throughout a piece, or a section of a piece. "Song Without Words" has a bass ostinato.

Song Without Words

By RICHARD BRADLEY

© 1996 BRADLEY PUBLICATIONS
All Rights Reserved

Lullaby Of Broadway

Music by
HARRY WARREN
Arranged by Richard Bradley

© 1935, 1950 WARNER BROS. INC.
This Arrangement © 1996 WARNER BROS. INC.
Copyright Renewed
All Rights Reserved

C
G7
C

G
E7/G♯
Am7
D7
G

E7/G♯
Am7
D7
G7

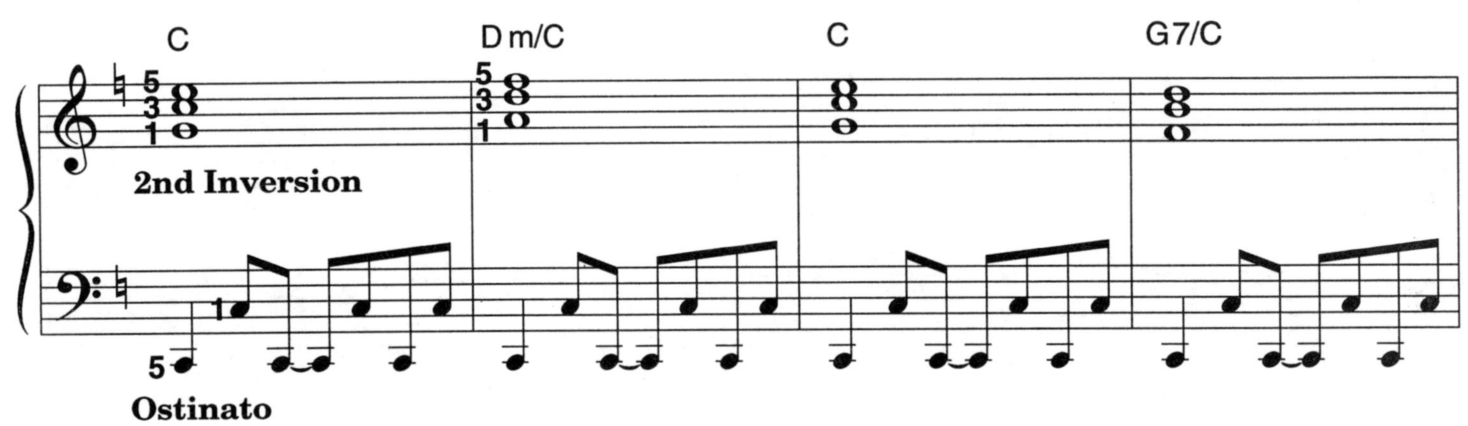
C
Dm/C
C
G7/C
2nd Inversion
Ostinato

C
Dm/C
C
G7/C
C
5
2
1
1st Inversion
C
5
3
1
Dm/C
C
G7/C
C
Dm/C
C
Dm
E♭m
Em
A♭7
f
3 1
3 4 1
Dm
C
Am
A♭7
G7
3 1
3 4 1
1
1
C6

Triplets

A **triplet** is three notes played in the time of two of the same kind of note. It is usually marked with a 3 above it, or with a 3 and a slur above it. Play the exercise below. Keep an even beat. Count the triplets either way they are marked.

Playing The Notes Of A Chord

Often, all of the notes of a chord are not played. This is especially true of seventh chords played in the bass where they can be too deep and muddy sounding.

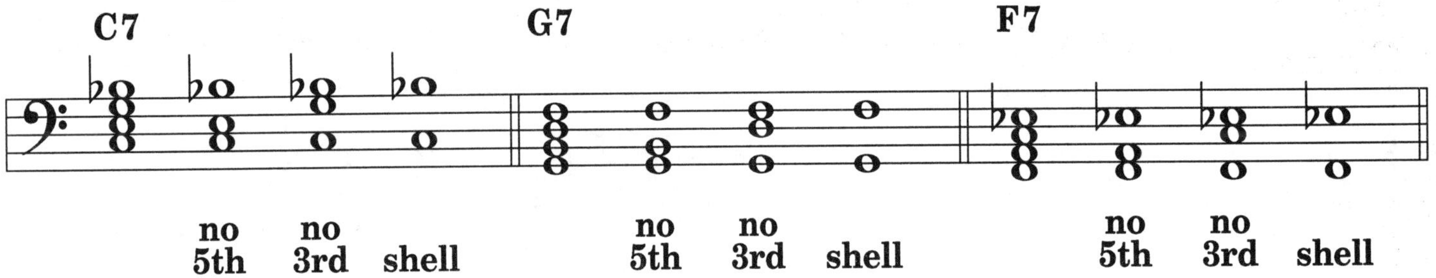

Playing The Blues In G

Look at the circle to the right. As with the C and F major scales, the V and IV chords are still neighbors of the I chord (still on each side of it).

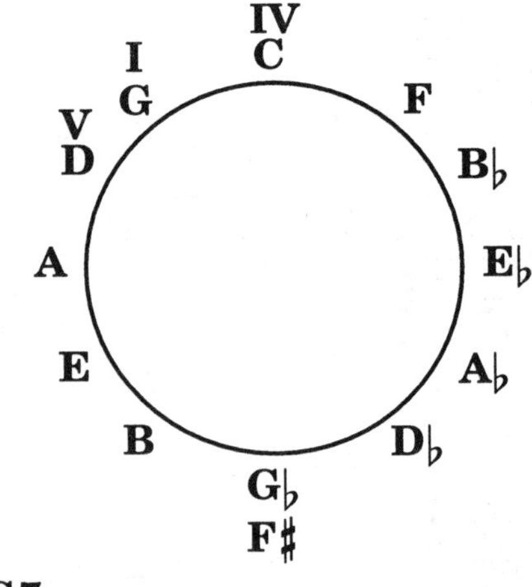

The following blues progression uses a IV7 chord in the second measure.

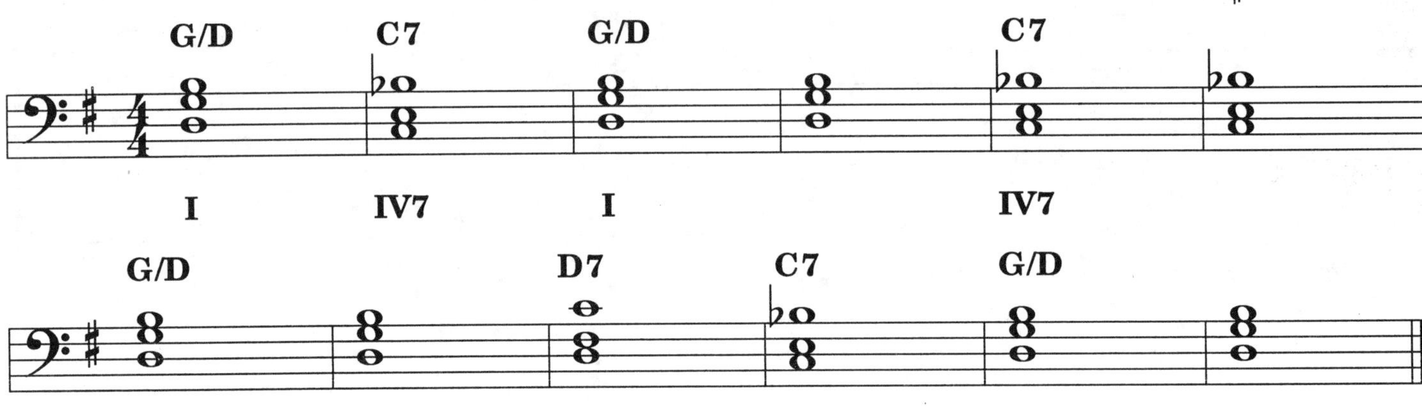

Memphis Bar - B - Q

By RICHARD BRADLEY

© 1996 BRADLEY PUBLICATIONS
All Rights Reserved

More Chords

The **augmented chord** raises the fifth of the chord one half step.
The chord symbol is the letter name plus either aug or +.

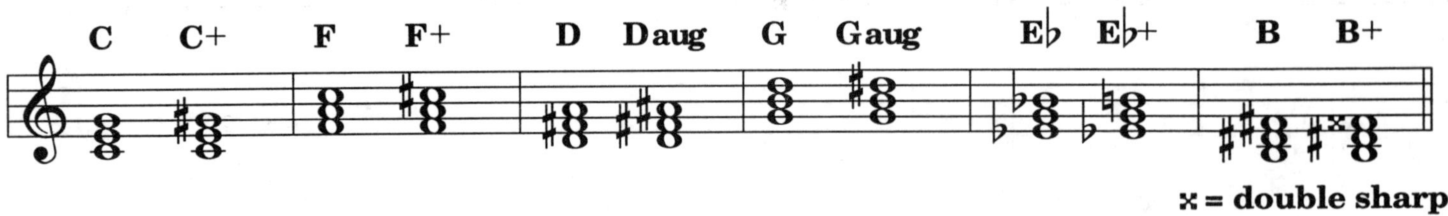

The **diminished chord** lowers both the third and the fifth one half step.
The chord symbol is the letter name plus dim or °.

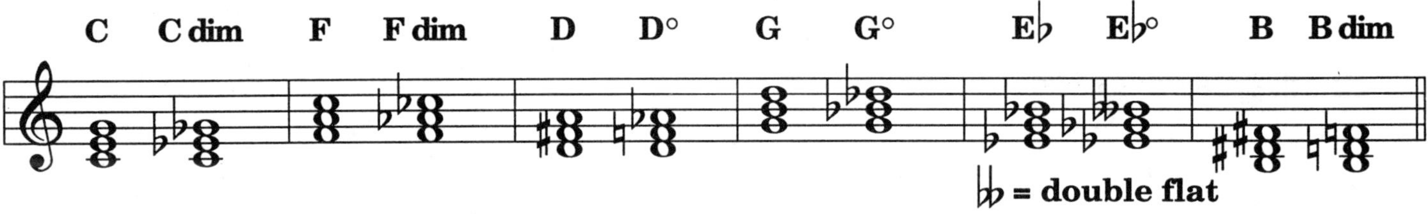

Combining chords with ones you already know creates many possibilities.

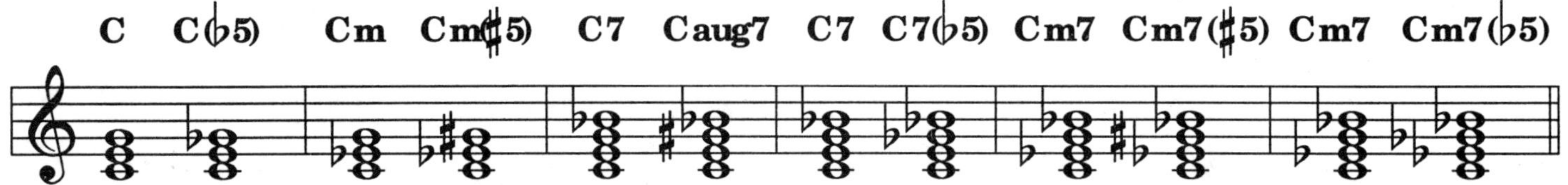

Complete the following chords:

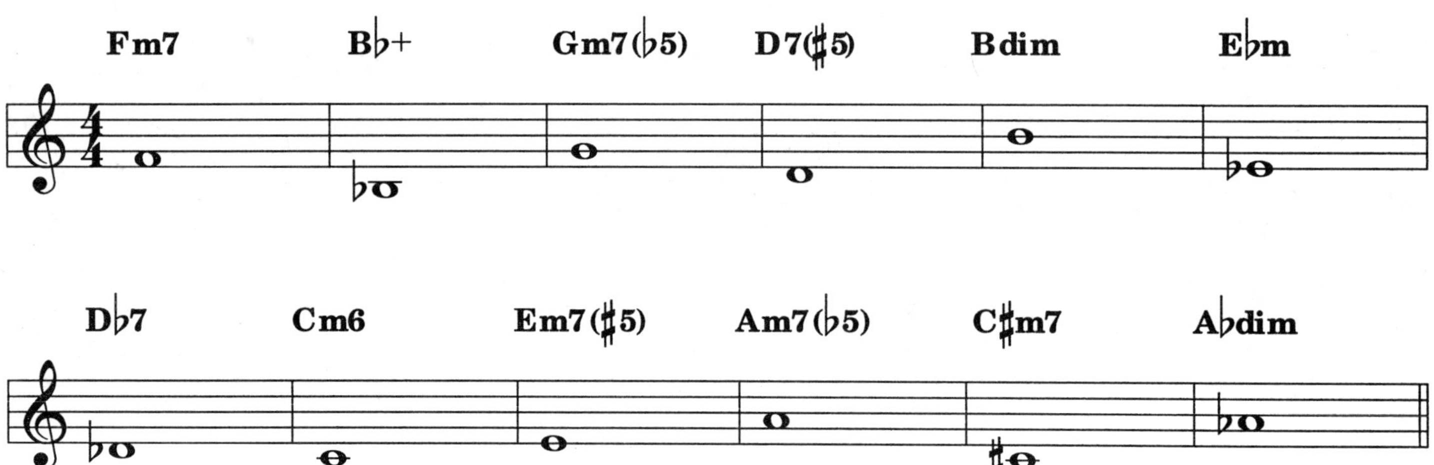

To play an **arpeggio**, play the notes of a chord one after the other instead of simultaneously. There is an example of a **short arpeggio** below. Play the left hand chord, then the right hand chord, then cross your left hand over for a single note. This harp-style effect makes wonderful fill-ins and endings.

C
Am
Dm
G
L.H.
L.H.
L.H.
L.H.
with pedal

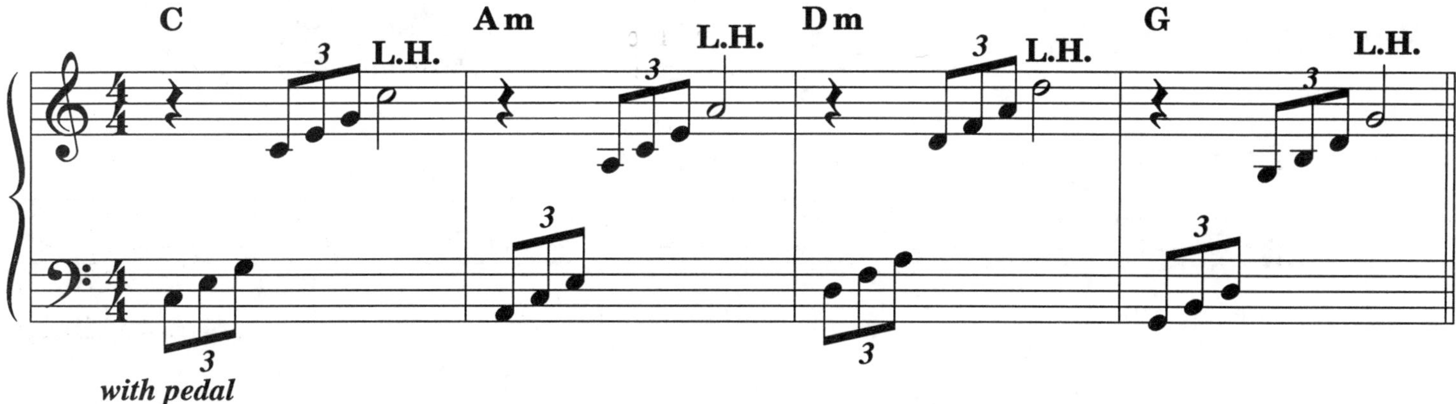

New Age Harp

By RICHARD BRADLEY

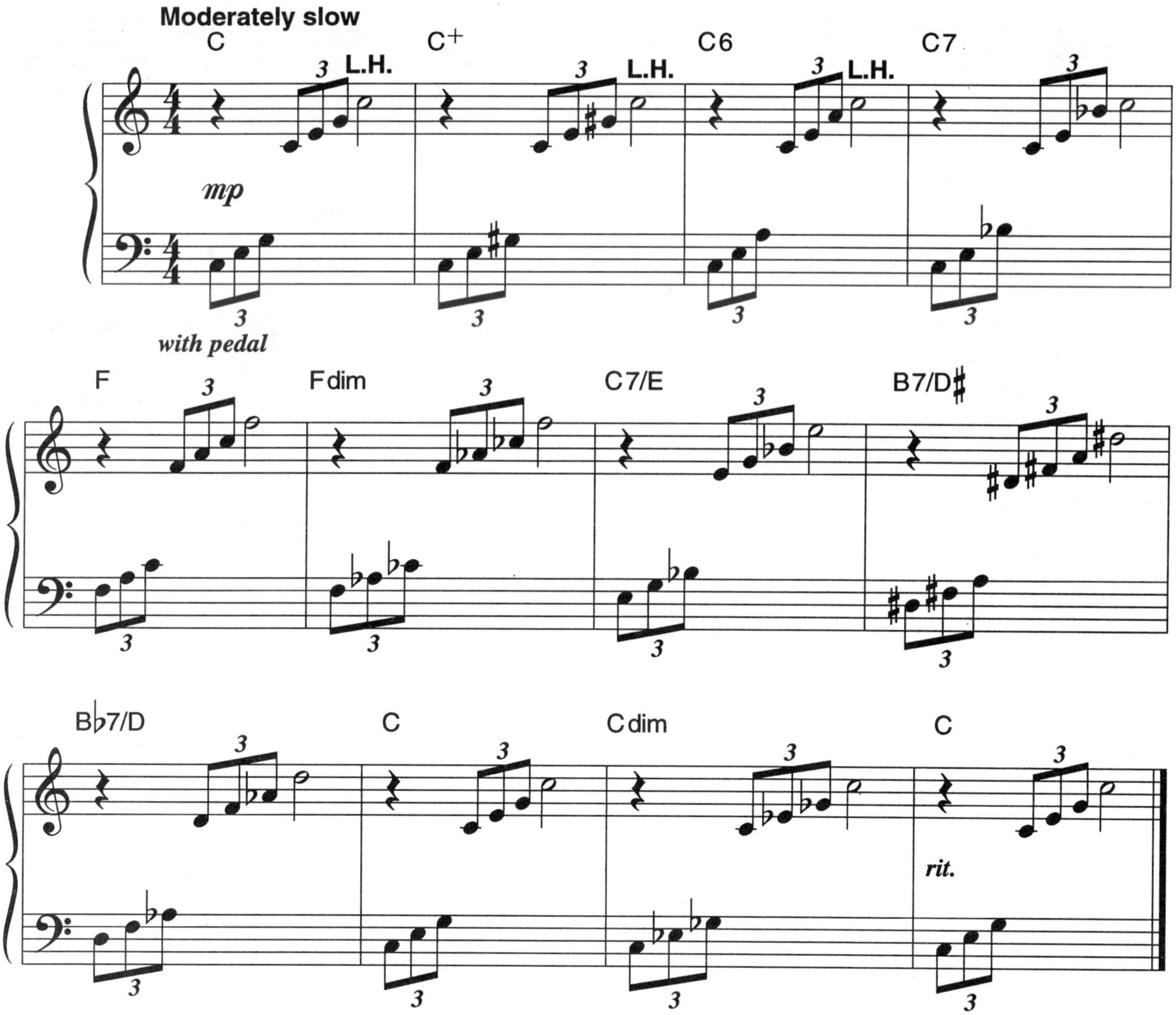

Moderately slow
C
C+
C6
C7
L.H.
L.H.
L.H.
mp
with pedal
F
Fdim
C7/E
B7/D♯
B♭7/D
C
Cdim
C
rit.

© 1996 BRADLEY PUBLICATIONS
All Rights Reserved

Ebb Tide

Words by
CARL SIGMAN

Music by
ROBERT MAXWELL
Arranged by Richard Bradley

© 1953 (Renewed 1981) ROBBINS MUSIC CORPORATION
All Rights of ROBBINS MUSIC CORPORATION Assigned to EMI CATALOGUE PARTNERSHIP
All Rights Administered by EMI ROBBINS CATALOG (Publishing) and WARNER BROS. PUBLICATIONS U.S., INC. (Print)
All Rights Reserved

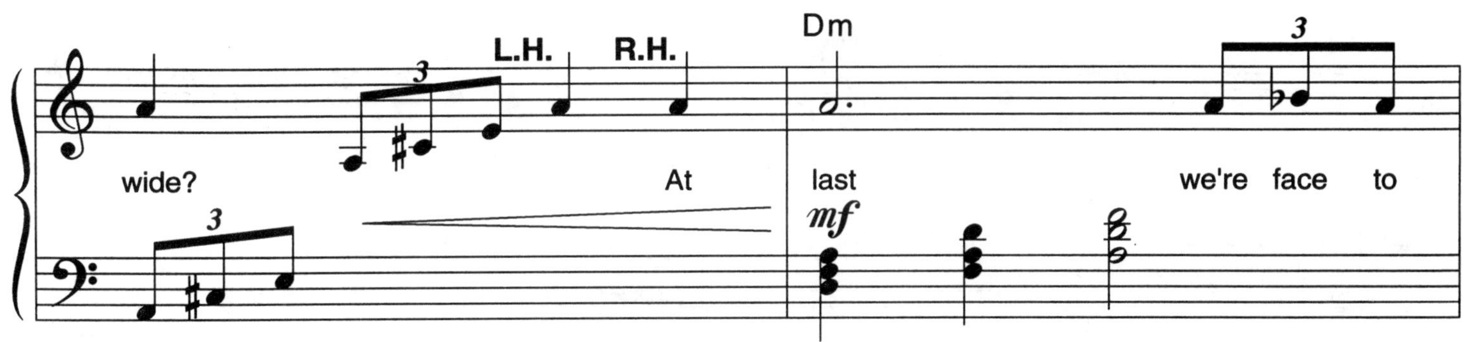
L.H.
R.H.
Dm
wide?
At
last
we're face to
mf

E
Am
face,
and as we
kiss
through an em -
cresc.

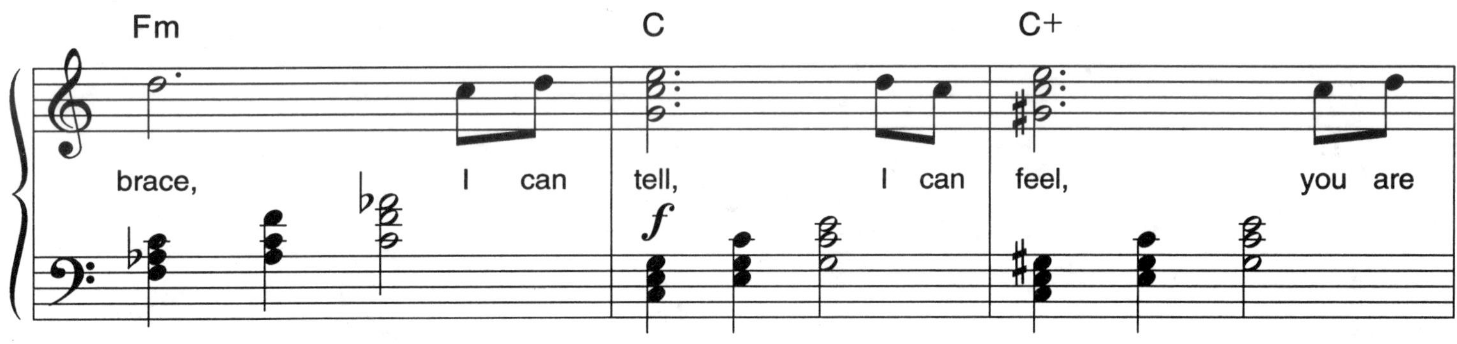
Fm
C
C+
brace,
I can
tell,
I can
feel,
you are
f

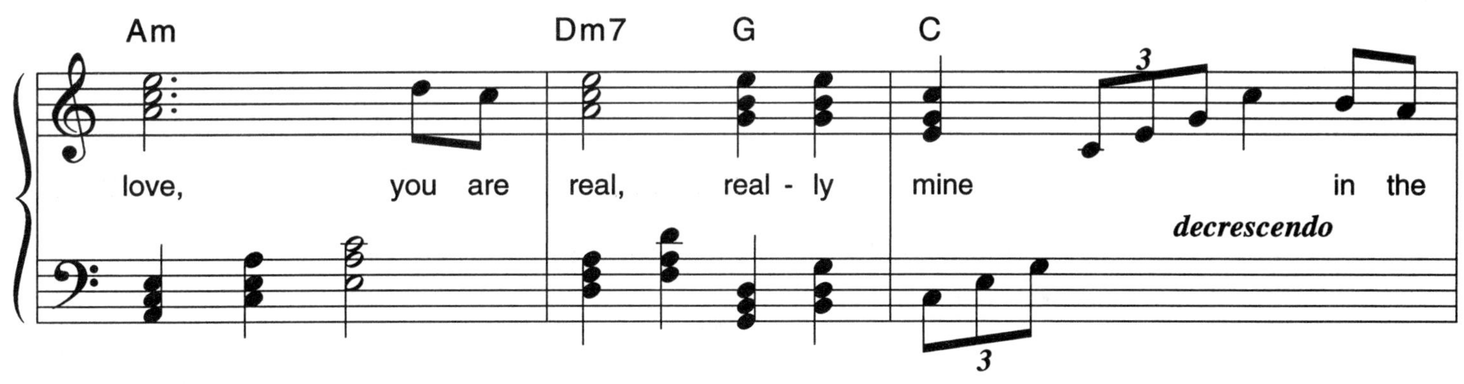
Am
Dm7
G
C
love,
you are
real,
real - ly
mine
in the
decrescendo

Am
Fm
rain,
in the
dark,
in the
Dm
G7
C
sun.
Like the
tide
at it's
Am
Dm
Fm
ebb,
I'm at
peace
in the
web
of your
C
arms.
L.H.
R.H.

Root – Fifth Rhythm Pattern

Using just the root and fifth of a chord creates a perfect rhythm for many types of music: jazz, country, polka, big band era, etc.

Play the root, fifth, fifth an octave lower, the back up to the fifth.

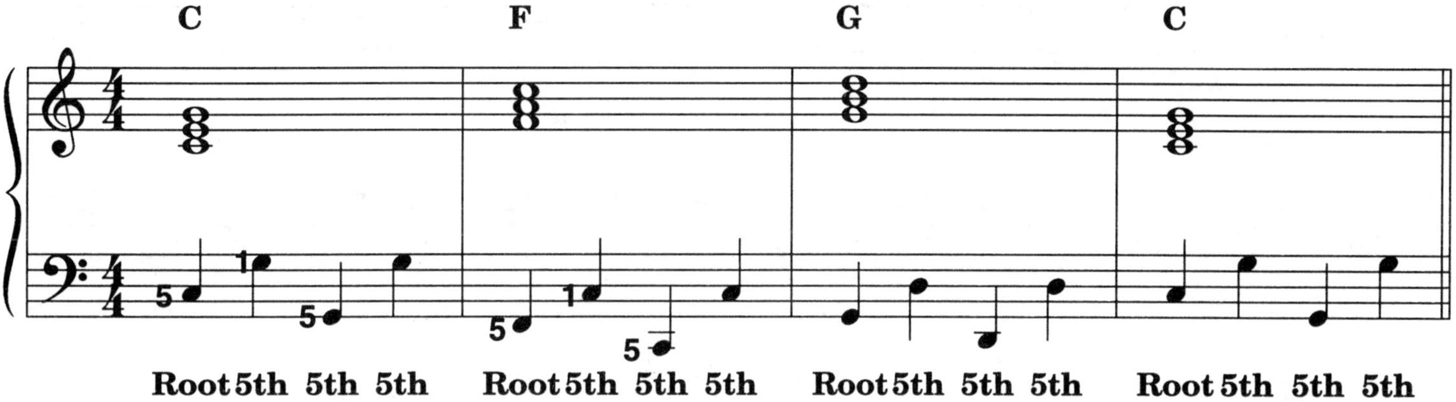

Play the example below using the root-fifth rhythm.

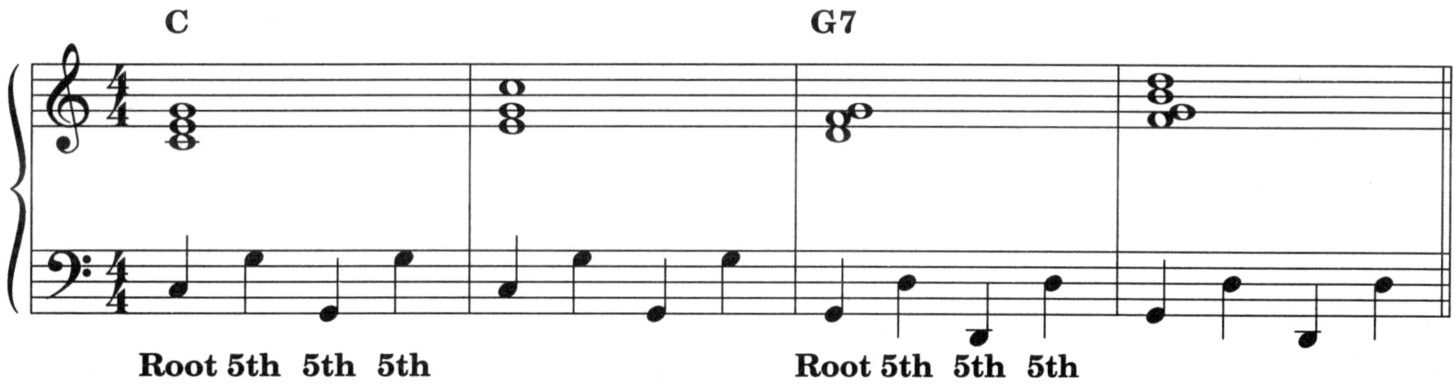

For smoother playing, we often play the fifth first then go to the root.
This is especially used on the V chord.

Glow Worm

By PAUL LINCKE
Arranged by Richard Bradley

© 1996 BRADLEY PUBLICATIONS
All Rights Reserved

Careless Love

TRADITIONAL
Arranged by Richard Bradley

© 1996 BRADLEY PUBLICATIONS
All Rights Reserved

Down By The Riverside

TRADITIONAL
Arranged by Richard Bradley

© 1996 BRADLEY PUBLICATIONS
All Rights Reserved

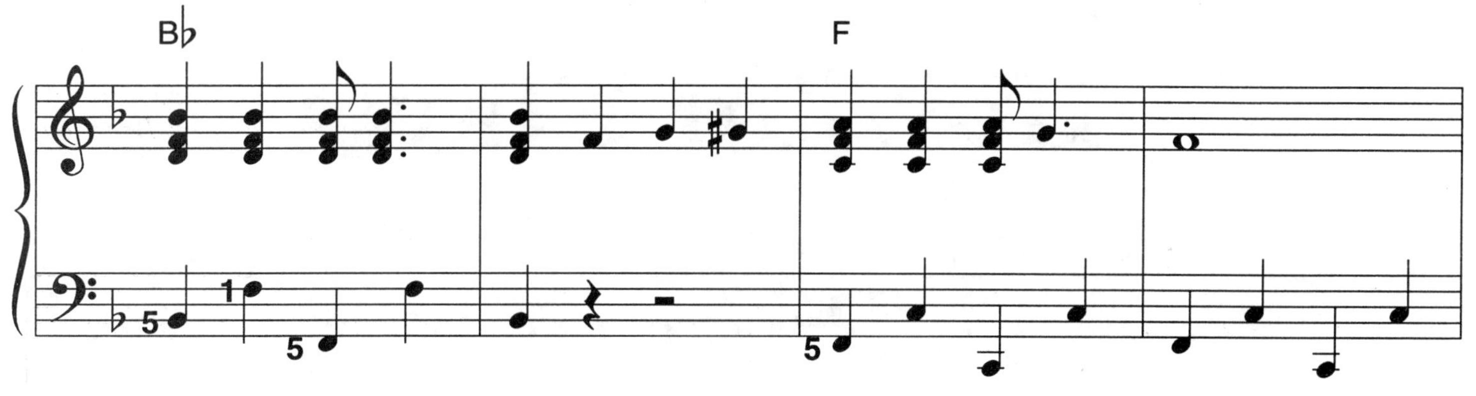
B♭
F
1
5
5
5

C7
F
F7
1
1

B♭
F

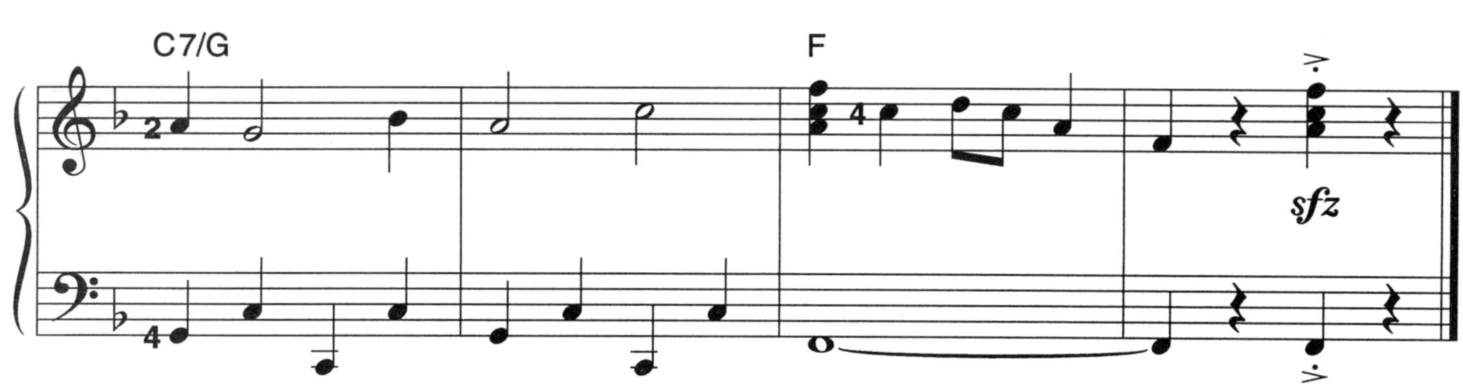
C7/G
F
2
4
4
sfz

Bradley's

How To Play *Pop and Jazz* Piano

by

Richard Bradley

Book Two:

Continuing Blues Progressions
The Complete Blues Scale
More Chords and Chord Progressions
More Improvisation Techniques
Playing From a Lead Line (Fake Book)
Rock Rhythms and Styles
Popular Piano Styles
Swing Style
Jazz Style Rhythms and Riffs

Book Three:

More Chord Progressions
Polychords
Jazz Riffs and Patterns
Quartal Harmony
Whole Tone Harmony
Jazz Scales
Piano Styles